Howling at the Moon

Walking the Pennine Way

John Davison

Howling at the Moon – Walking the Pennine Way

First edition, 2017.

© John Davison, 2017.

The right of John Davison to be identified as the author of this work has been asserted by him in accordance with the Copyright, Designs and Patents Act, 1988.

All rights reserved. No part of this publication may be reproduced, stored in a retrieval system, or transmitted, in any form or by any means without the prior written permission of the publisher, nor be otherwise circulated in any form of binding or cover other than that in which it is published and without a similar condition being imposed on the subsequent purchaser.

Cover photograph: Barn at Malham, North Yorkshire, © John Davison, 2017.

For Charlotte and Thomas

Contents

Part 1

Chapter 1 – Preparations   1

Chapter 2 – The Dry Run   30

Chapter 3 – Committed   52

Chapter 4 – The Peak District   54

Chapter 5 – The South Pennines   63

Chapter 6 – The Yorkshire Dales   75

Chapter 7 – The North Pennines   93

Chapter 8 – Northumberland   121

Part 2

Chapter 9 – Trail Facts   139

Chapter 10 – Route Assessment   143

Chapter 11 – Route Data   151

Index   165

Part 1

Chapter 1

Preparations

The concept. – Planning it out. – Lightweight backpacking. – Trekking pole pros and cons. – A rucksack that fights back. – One man's need to contribute to society.

*****

From: Jeff
Sent: 31 January, 07:21
To: John
Subject: Epiphany!!

Hi John.

I've had a moment. You could call it a midlife crisis but I've had the affairs and bought the sports cars.

I've decided to walk the Pennine Way in May. No namby-pamby, hoity-toity to and from point to point. This is hard-core, balding man, howling at the moon nonsense!!

I've decided to "find myself" whatever that means and do the walk in one hit, complete – idiot style!! Take whatever comes, adapt and overcome!

I've quit my job after being asked by a twenty-something CEO (daddy's company) to "sell myself" to him.

If you have done this walk I would appreciate advice. I have one piece currently awaiting publication and would like to produce an idiot's blog as it would appeal to 50 something men. I would appreciate any advice if you have done this walk.

Jeff

*****

From:	John
Sent:	01 February, 11:49
To:	Jeff
Subject:	Re: Epiphany!!

Hi Jeff.

Good for you! "Sell yourself"? FFS!

I haven't walked the whole Pennine Way. Just a short section near Edale and an even shorter bit where it crosses the Coast to Coast, but I know that it's supposed to be quite bleak countryside. From the little I've seen of the Pennines, I find that an attraction rather than a drawback. The PW is known for being boggy, but I think the boggiest sections now have flagstone paths so shouldn't be as tricky as they used to be. It looks a superb walk. Stick "High Cup" into Google Images and see.

If you're backpacking, I'd recommend that you go as lightweight as possible.

Preparations

Start by weighing every item and log the weights on a spreadsheet so that you create a "master" gear list.

Then, I'd carry out an assessment of the route. What temperatures and wind speeds can you expect? Is rain likely? How often? And so on, and so on.

Using the route assessment and your master gear list, work out what items you'll need, switching in lighter items and checking the weight as you do so. Take exactly what you'll need for the conditions you'll encounter; don't weigh yourself down with toot.

Then research the route in terms of facilities (pubs, food shops, campsites, etc.). For instance, you can cut down the amount of food you'll need to carry if you know exactly where all the shops and pubs are, and what times they open.

I can't over-emphasise the link between a light load on your back and your enjoyment of the trip. When I walked the Anglesey Coastal Path last year, I chatted with a walker who was carrying, so he told me, an 80lb pack. 80lbs! I was carrying 12lbs for the same walk. He had sore hips, sore knees and a sore back. I didn't. I struggle to describe the difference in our attitudes and approaches to backpacking, but I bet my journey was more enjoyable than his. He had done no research on his route and he was carrying a week's worth of food – and this on a path where you are never more than a couple of days from a food shop!

The Pennine Way has long been on my bucket list so if you'd like a +1 for this gig, let me know. I realise that's a bit cheeky and I totally understand if you need to do it alone. I'll help all I can whichever you decide.

Howling at the Moon

Good luck, mate!

John

*****

From:	Jeff
Sent:	01 February, 14:53
To:	John
Subject:	Re: Epiphany!!

Thanks for such a comprehensive approach. It is really appreciated.

The Pennine Way is one of those challenges just begging for one to give it a crack and due to the distance and time needed to complete it, I reckon it will provide some great experiences – good and not so good.

Of course, you are more than welcome to come along.

Jeff

*****

From:	John
Sent:	02 February, 12:25
To:	Jeff
Subject:	Cornwall Coast Path

Jeff,

I was planning to hike part of the coast path in Cornwall in April. Just a few days to stretch my legs and try out a few new items of kit. Nothing too strenuous.

Preparations

Do you fancy joining me? If yes, we could use the Cornish walk as a dry run for the Pennine Way.

John

*****

From: Jeff
Sent: 02 February, 13:11
To: John
Subject: Re: Cornwall Coast Path

Sounds good matey. Let me know when you are planning to do it.

Jeff

*****

From: John
Sent: 02 February, 14:34
To: Jeff
Subject: Re: Cornwall Coast Path

Jeff,

My plan is:

18th April
Train to Hayle. Walk out of Hayle along the coast path.

19th – 21st April
Walk around the coast path to Penzance. Wild camp as necessary.

22nd April
Train home.

The whole walk totals 75km long (about 45 miles), so we wouldn't be walking a huge distance each day.

John

*****

From: John
Sent: 04 February, 13:38
To: Jeff
Subject: Lightweight gear

Hi Jeff,

I've sent you some links on lightweight backpacking gear.

The easiest way to make a big weight-saving is to get lightweight versions of "the big three", i.e. your rucksack, tent and sleeping bag (+mat). If you can get these things down to less than three kilos in total then you're well on your way, so concentrate on rucksacks, tents and sleeping bags as you browse. You'll need to know the weights of your existing kit first, of course, in order to make a comparison.

To give an idea, the tent, rucksack, sleeping bag and mat which I'll probably bring on the Pennine Way total 2.5kg, and that lot will keep me very warm, very dry and very comfortable.

John

*****

Preparations

From: Jeff
Sent: 04 February, 14:11
To: John
Subject: Re: Lightweight gear

Thanks John,

I need to revisit the old rucksack saga and get a lighter one that will not fight me every time I put it on, and a new sleeping bag.

Jeff

*****

From: John
Sent: 15 February, 21:54
To: Jeff
Subject: Cornish Coast Path

Jeff,

Our train leaves Paddington at 1006, so I'd suggest we meet at the entrance to Platform 8 at, say, 0930?

We arrive in Hayle at 1454.

Do we need to speak on kit and food or are you OK on that?

BTW, if you want to take the relevant OS map, it's Landranger 203. If you don't want to buy one, I have a spare copy (1992 vintage).

John

Howling at the Moon

*****

From: Jeff
Sent: 16 February, 10:20
To: John
Subject: Re: Cornish Coast Path

No worries, it all makes sense. I'll sort my tickets and meet you as suggested. I think I'll stay with my current kit for this walk. I've got this weird idea that carrying heavier kit will be a good workout as well as a walk. I did it for Hadrian's Wall and although a challenge it was a sense of achievement knowing that I completed 90-odd miles with, I would estimate, 10-15kg (yes, I reckon I took the kitchen sink as well – never used half of it either!!).

I'll grab an OS map at my local bookshop as I need the practice of map reading. I do have one of those super-duper GPS thingys as well which I've only used once. I can download the route on it. Might as well reacquaint myself with that too.

Have you got one of your itineraries for this walk? Thought you sent one but cannot find it.

Jeff

*****

From: John
Sent: 17 February, 17:56
To: Jeff
Subject: Re: Cornish Coast Path

Jeff,

Preparations

Paperwork for the Cornish Coast Path attached.

Good idea re the map and GPS. I was thinking about bringing a GPS on the Pennine Way to help with route finding. I think one might be useful, particularly in very bad weather. The Cornish Coast Path should be easy: providing the sea is on our right, we're doing OK. But a safe environment in which to practice nonetheless.

I love the "I would estimate 10-15kg". I'm weighing my stuff to the nearest gram and you're accurate to the nearest 5kg! I need to lighten up (mentally, I mean).

See you at Paddington.

John

*****

From: Jeff
Sent: 17 February, 07:42
To: John
Subject: Re: Cornish Coast Path

I dare say if I had been on as many walks as you, I'd be more circumspect regarding weight. I'm still at the naïve stage where weight = good stamina workout in addition to aerobic training through walking undulating terrain.

You remind me of my neighbour who is really into his cycling and replaces parts on his cycle with super-duper, state of the art lightweight alloys saving one gram here and a couple of grams there, thinking it will make him faster – I've told him if he drops a few kgs in body weight he would go faster without the huge expense!!! (Not that I think you should lose weight!!)

Howling at the Moon

I really need to use my GPS and was also thinking of using the Cornish trail as a dry run for the Pennine Way just to get to know it. I've got the card with full UK mapping but never used it!

Jeff

*****

From: John
Sent: 17 February, 23:31
To: Jeff
Subject: Re: Cornish Coast Path

Here's a thought, then. Just running it up the flagpole to see if anyone salutes it in a blue-sky-thinking sort of way.

Do you fancy carrying my stuff too?

You'd get an even better stamina workout and I'd go as lightweight as it's possible to go (carrying zero).

I realise that would probably lead to us walking at different speeds but, if you're agreeable, I reckon I could speed things up with some moderately foul language and a stick with a nail in the end.

Come on, admit you're tempted!

*****

From: Jeff
Sent: 18 February, 08:31
To: John

Subject: Re: Cornish Coast Path

I think you are asking me to be a Sherpa? I'm just naïve over weight. You wait – after a day or two on the Pennine Way I'll have discarded kit, use a bin bag as a tent and wash in puddles!!

Will book train ticket today – rucksack being taken by Fedex using a Hercules transport aircraft.

Walking poles – are they a good thing or just for old gits who can't hack it on dodgy knees?

*****

From: John
Sent: 18 February, 16:15
To: Jeff
Subject: Re: Cornish Coast Path

Walking poles? I find them really useful. Not least because one of them doubles as the pole for my tent.

I didn't get on with the first set of poles I tried. Too much faff taking them on and off my wrists every time I wanted to look at the map or take a photo. Nick borrowed the poles to try them out and it was no great loss to me when he broke them. No great surprise either, if you've ever done anything with Nick.

Then I tried again, a different make, and I became a convert. Less stress on my legs, more stability when I need it and better posture.

I've just booked my ticket to Hayle. Will your rucksack be coming with us on the train or will it require a train of its own?

*****

From:	Jeff
Sent:	18 February, 16:38
To:	John
Subject:	Re: Cornish Coast Path

Ha!! I'm still trying to sweet-talk it into coming along. Hopefully we'll have no fights when I try to put it on this time!!

*****

From:	John
Sent:	19 February, 14:46
To:	Jeff
Subject:	Re: Cornish Coast Path

I reckon they'll need to sedate that rucksack before they try to get it onto a plane. Or try to coax it on board with food.

J.

*****

From:	Jeff
Sent:	19 February, 14:46
To:	John
Subject:	Re: Cornish Coast Path

Just looked at poles online – alloy or carbon? This is all very techie and if it's just about saving 0.0000005g weight on a trek or being 0.0000001% more aerodynamic, I'll just eat one less pork pie and shave my legs to improve slipstream!

*****

Preparations

From: John
Sent: 19 February, 15:23
To: Jeff
Subject: Re: Cornish Coast Path

I'll remind you of that reckless commitment to eat one less pork pie when we're out on the Pennine moors.

I think my poles are carbon, but alloys would do just as well. Cheap or expensive, it doesn't really matter, but they will help you on a long walk.

I've just invested in a set of three maps covering the Pennine Way.

*****

From: Jeff
Sent: 19 February, 15:41
To: John
Subject: Re: Cornish Coast Path

Really in two minds whether to get poles, they just seem a faff and an admission one is getting old!! I may try the Cornish Walk without and reconsider for the Pennine Way – they might be more useful for the distance – that will be the issue!

Those maps are really good, I used one for Hadrian's Wall (not for map reading as you can't miss the bloody thing!) and they are very sturdy and take all sorts of abuse (bit like my rucksack…)

*****

From: John
Sent: 19 February, 17:17
To: Jeff
Subject: Re: Cornish Coast Path

Wise decision re the poles, I think. People can rave about them but they have to be right for you. You can always come over for dinner and give mine a try.

*****

From: Jeff
Sent: 19 February, 17:42
To: John
Subject: Re: Cornish Coast Path

I thought so too but just had a rush of blood to the head and ordered a pair (can always sell them on if I can't get on with them). Dinner sometime would be good – can always practice with them on the stairs or yomping around the garden!

*****

SMS message: 23/02, 12:41
From: John

Pennine Way map set just arrived!

*****

SMS message: 23/02, 12:48
From: Jeff

I need to order mine. Are you going to memorise them so you don't need to carry them and save 0.0000005g (dependent upon

Preparations

the lunar position and gravitational pull) on the trail?

My "old man" walking poles arrived today. Will have to practice in the dark with a disguise in case I'm recognised. They look well-built mind.

*****

SMS message: 23/02, 12:55
From: John

I admit that in the past I have stored docs on my phone to save weight. But I'm sure the poles will help you.

*****

SMS message: 23/02, 12:58
From: Jeff

I'll be able to trial them properly in Cornwall – see if they can fight off grizzly bears on the moors!!

*****

SMS message: 24/02, 17:07

John, do you remember Tony? He's interested in the coastal path walk. Can he come along?

*****

SMS message: 24/02, 17:16

Of course, mate. Just give him the time and date to meet us at Hayle or Paddington, whichever he prefers. Let him know it

Howling at the Moon

won't be too testing. About 25km/day max.

*****

SMS message: 24/02, 17:59
From: Jeff

Done that. Thanks.

*****

From: John
Sent: 01 March, 14:08
To: Jeff
Subject: Food for Cornish Coast Path

Jeff,

I've been thinking about our food for the Cornish Coast Path.

We start on the Monday. I'm assuming we'll eat sandwiches or something similar on the train, then we arrive in Hayle just after 3pm. St Ives is 10km from Hayle so we could walk to St Ives and have dinner in a pub there. It would set us up nicely and save carrying an extra meal. After dinner we can walk out of town along the coast path and find a quiet field to sleep in.

Our last day is Friday and I'm assuming we'll get breakfast in Penzance before heading home.

That means we'll need to carry three breakfasts, three lunches, three dinners and any drinks and snacks we need.

What do you think?

Preparations

John

*****

From: Jeff
Sent: 01 March, 15:31
To: John
Subject: Re: Food for Cornish Coast Path

Hi John,

I like the thinking here. Sounds OK to me. I also like your thoughts on the Pennine Way too. Sorry I've been quiet, been a bit preoccupied trying to secure what could be a nice little part-time consultancy number. It's like tickling trout to make them bite (I kid you not!!)

No idea if Tony is coming on the coastal walk. Mind you, last Wednesday we got absolutely bladdered – I haven't drunk like that for years and am in the middle of a low carb diet so had an empty stomach too (schoolboy error). I cannot even remember how I got home. We ended up in a pub in Kensington (God knows why as we started off in east London) and I haven't heard from Tony since. I'll give him a ring tonight.

Jeff

*****

From: John
Sent: 01 March, 16:55
To: Jeff
Subject: Re: Food for Cornish Coast Path

I'm impressed with your homing instincts while under the

influence – might be useful up on the moors.

That Pennine Way stuff took a lot of time to put together. I haven't decided whether it would be better to re-stock with food from the various small shops along the way or to post food parcels ahead (or a combination of the two). Parcelforce let me down badly on the Offa's Dyke Path, so I've gone right off the food parcel idea. There are just too many ways for it to go wrong and Parcelforce are working hard to discover new ones all the time.

That said, it's not much fun loading up with stuff at the local Spar shop and then having to get out of the rain in a bus shelter while I re-package it all in my rucksack. That might be the lesser of two evils, though. And I think we'll be able to get a lot of meals in pubs and cafés, which will take the pressure off.

I'm going to try freezer bag cooking on the Cornish trip and, if I get on well with it, I'll probably do it on the Pennine Way too.

For example, I start with something like instant noodles or quick-cook pasta. Empty the contents into a zip-lock freezer bag and discard the packaging (to save weight).

Then, when I want a meal, I take the freezer bag with the pasta or noodles in it, place it in an insulating cosy (like an envelope but made from foil-covered bubble wrap), add boiling water and let it stand for a few minutes. Add a sachet of tuna or a few slices of corned beef or ham and away you go. The cosy keeps the food warm while it re-hydrates, so I don't need to burn gas simmering it for ages and thus I don't need to carry lots of fuel.

And, I hope, it shouldn't be too difficult to get noodles and pasta in little shops.

Preparations

John

*****

From: Jeff
Sent: 02 March, 0910
To: John
Subject: Re: Food for Cornish Coast Path

Well impressive, John. It will be interesting to see how you get on with the freezer bag cooking. I'll plump for traditional freeze dried meals. It will be an interesting contrast.

I must admit doing all the postal malarkey for the Pennine Way seems a bit of a faff, it's not as if we are miles away from food and water throughout.

Jeff

*****

From: John
Sent: 02 March, 09:57
To: Jeff
Subject: Re: Food for Cornish Coast Path

Not my ideas, old chap. I'm borrowing from others here. "Standing on the shoulders of giants", as Isaac Newton put it.

I posted two food parcels ahead before walking the Offa's Dyke Path, both addressed to me at Post Offices. They usually hold your mail for you when you do that (it's called *poste restante*) – I've used it before and never had a problem. Imagine how I felt when I found that neither of my parcels had been delivered. My, how I chuckled! In one case Parcelforce had tried to deliver the parcel to the Post Office when the office was closed, and so they left one of their "You were out when we tried to deliver your parcel" cards. At a Post Office! As you can imagine, the Post Office staff did *not* charge off to the Parcelforce depot waving their card and remembering to take ID.

I think the problem stems from the privatisation and splitting up of the Royal Mail and Parcelforce. Letter and parcel delivery are now done by two separate and very different companies.

Anyway, after Parcelforce let me down I bought stuff from local shops and used a pot cosy to cook it. It's the same principle as freezer bag cooking but, instead of a plastic bag, you put the food into your cooking pot, add boiling water, place the pot into a pot cosy to insulate it and let the whole thing stand for a while. The one downside is that, unlike freezer bag cooking, you now have a pot to wash up. But it worked well on the Offa's Dyke trip.

Duct tape, loft insulation, an hour's work and a few quid to Homebase.

John

*****

From: John
Sent: 07 March, 11:51
To: Jeff
Subject: Thinking ahead

Jeff,

Preparations

I've been doing some thinking about meal planning for the Pennine Way an I thought I'd share it with you in case it's of use.

Firstly, I've assumed that we're likely to walk a minimum of 25km per day. I expect we'll sometimes do more than that, but it's a reasonable figure to use for planning.

Secondly, as we discussed, I've assumed that we will be re-supplying from shops and not posting food parcels ahead.

Then I've used the data sheet I prepared to work out how far we're likely to have to walk between food shops.

I've concluded that if we carry three days' worth of food when we start at Edale, that will see us through to Hebden Bridge. After that we should be able to re-supply at a food shop every two or three days (Hebden Bridge, Gargrave, Hawes, Middleton-in-Teesdale, Alston, Bellingham and on to the end of the walk at Kirk Yetholm).

I think the attractions of this approach are:

- We never have to carry more than three days' food at any one time. Even if we "go large" and carry a kilo of food per day (and that would be a lot of food) that would still only amount to a maximum of 3kg of food carried at any one time. That's eminently do-able.

- The shops where I've aimed to re-supply are open 0700-2200, seven days a week, so the chances are that they will be open when we pass them.

- There are a few other (very small) shops where we

might be able to top up in an emergency.

If we get the occasional pub meal we can carry even less, or work with a safety margin of food.

What do you think?

John

PS Dates? I've got a family commitment at the beginning of May and another at the end, so the 4th or 5th would be good start dates for me. Any good for you?

*****

From: John
Sent: 03 March, 18:28
To: Jeff
Subject: Book on way to you

Jeff,

I've been re-reading an old book called, *Journey Through Britain*, by John Hillaby, a prodigious walker. It's long out of print, but I've found a second-hand copy for peanuts and it's on its way to you. It's one of my favourite books, but that's not why I've got you a copy.

The book is Hillaby's account of his walk from Land's End to John O'Groats in 1968. I'd forgotten that during this epic hike he walked the length of the Pennine Way. I've found it fascinating ticking off the names of places I checked out when I was doing the research for our walk. When Hillaby did it, the Pennine Way was just a few years old and the towns and villages along the route were still industrial cloth-making and weaving towns.

If it's not your thing, don't worry. But do have a look at Chapters 9-12 (the Pennine Way ones). Hillaby must have been hitting his stride by the time he reached the PW, because he completed it in just 11 days!

J.

*****

From: Jeff
Sent: 08 March, 11:20
To: John
Subject: Re: Book on way to you

Hi John,

Received the book.

Thanks.

Jeff.

*****

SMS message: 18/03, 10:29
From: John

Jeff, to help me plan my life, can we start the Pennine Way on 4th or 5th May?

*****

SMS message: 18/03, 11:19

Howling at the Moon

From: Jeff

I've got no firm commitments at work that impact, so I'm ok with that.

*****

SMS message: 18/03, 12:28
From: John

Excellent! Let's say 4th May then.

*****

SMS message: 18/03, 12:31
From: Jeff

How many days do you estimate?

*****

SMS message: 18/03, 13:02
From: John

Hmm. Difficult to say. Most people reckon 2-3 weeks. It's 423km long.

*****

SMS message: 18/03, 13:08
From: Jeff

Knew it was a challenge but do-able with a bit of determination, I should think (been increasing my fitness training in anticipation). Should be quite an experience.

Preparations

*****

From: John
Sent: 09 April, 12:12
To: Jeff
Subject: Hi Jeff

Hi Jeff,

Sorry I haven't been in touch (I've had nothing much to say, really) and glad your new work looks good. I assume from the salary that you've become a premiership footballer?!

Just got to get some food together and chuck a few things into my rucksack, and I'm all ready for the Cornish trip. And very much looking forward to it – it's been a long, grey winter and it will be good to be outdoors again! Three days' food should do us, I think. If we happen to pass a pub that serves food at a time when they're serving it, that will be a bonus.

As this is only a short trip I'm thinking about pre-booking the train home to get the cheaper fare. On 22nd the 0844 train from Penzance looks a good pick (and £67 from there to my local station). What do you think?

John

PS See you at Paddington. On the 18th **near the gate to Platform 8, train leaves at 1006!**

*****

From: Jeff
Sent: 09 April, 14:12

To: John
Subject: Re: Hi Jeff

Hi John,

Looking forward to it very much. Need to check my gear this weekend and untether my stroppy rucksack!!

It has been a rubbish winter and totally agree with travel suggestion.

A lot of this touting for work malarkey doesn't come to much and I think most of them only talk to me because I'm cheap! I should get a proper job but not a lot out there for unskilled over-50s.

Jeff

*****

From: John
Sent: 09 April, 15:28
To: Jeff
Subject: Re: Hi Jeff

I know what you mean, but in your situation do you really need a "proper job"? Maybe we only worked at all because we were born poor and had no other option? After all, we're only here once and our days are precious.

*****

From: Jeff
Sent: 09 April, 14:12
To: John

Preparations

Subject: Re: Hi Jeff

Good discussion to be had on our walk. It's not just about the money, it's about pride and still contributing to society. 55 is no age to sit on one's arse. I have tried to convince myself I could bury myself in books and study for a doctorate or sit down and construct mountain bikes (I am a qualified mechanic) or even take up golf or fishing but it's not me. Maybe it's an attitude I need to address. It would certainly make life a lot less complicated.

*****

From: John
Sent: 09 April, 16:35
To: Jeff
Subject: Re: Hi Jeff

I'll look forward to that!

What do you think about booking a ticket home from Penzance on the Friday? Discounted price for buying early and the 0844 train looks good.

*****

SMS message, 11/04, 19:44
From: Jeff

Hey dude! Was reading your Cornish coastal route summary and you describe some of the route as challenging. How challenging? You mention some tough cliff bits. I take it we will not be climbing difficult cliffs. I don't have a good head for sheer drops, especially if I have to hang on to one! Call me old fashioned but I quite like to keep my bones intact…

*****

SMS message, 11/04, 19:59
From: John

No climbing, mate. I think they wrote that for families and grannies.

*****

SMS message: 15/04, 07:56
From: Jeff

Back from Birmingham job interview. Seemed to go well but lots of competitors! Haven't had the time to check my tent by pitching it in the garden for next week and it's pissing down today (sure it will be fine). See you Monday!

*****

SMS message: 17/04, 14:31
From: Jeff

Hi John. My train arrives at Liverpool St at 9.09am and then it's the infamous Circle Line to Paddington.

*****

SMS message: 18/04, 09:02
From: Jeff

Amazingly at Paddington Station – no hitches anywhere! But we are leaving from Waterloo, I hear you say… I'll be on the main concourse with the incredibly uncooperative rucksack –

Preparations

you can't miss me…

*****

SMS message: 18/04, 09:24
From: John

Coincidence! Your rucksack just texted me to say it would be the rucksack on the concourse with the incredibly uncooperative owner!

*****

Chapter 2

The Dry Run

Cornwall. – Getting enough to eat. – Standing stones, spies and ships. – Signs of a storm brewing. – Running onto the Runnel. – The result of the dry run.

The South-West Coast Path is England's longest footpath. 1,014km in length, it runs from Minehead in Somerset, around Land's End, and along the south coast to Poole Harbour. The coast was patrolled by coastguards on foot right up until 1913 and it was their patrolling which established the path that has since become a National Trail.

Jeff and I weren't planning to walk all of the coast path. We had a short, 75km section marked out for our attention. We would, in effect, be walking a large letter "C", starting in Hayle on the north Cornish coast (the top end of the "C"), hiking around through Land's End and back (along the bottom part of the "C") to finish our walk in Penzance. By the end of our "dry run" we should, I hoped, be familiar with our kit and with each other's company. If any item failed or proved superfluous, or if we grated on each other, we should be able to identify the problem and resolve it before we set out on the longer and much more ambitious Pennine Way a few weeks later.

*****

The Dry Run

Our train pulled into Hayle Station exactly on time and was gone again before we'd found our way off of the platform.

The station was in a part of the town called "Foundry", named after the foundry and engineering works set up there by John Harvey, a local blacksmith, in 1779. Harvey's supplied the Cornish mining industry with steam-driven beam engines to pump water out of the deep levels. In their day, Harvey engines were exported all over the world and this area must have been a hive of activity. Now it sits quietly, apart from the traffic racing along the B road, for all the world as if waiting for something.

The former existence of Harvey's was the only thing I knew about Hayle before I went there. As we walked through Foundry and crossed the B-road to get onto the coast path I reflected that my knowledge appeared to be about 200 years out of date.

Despite my thirst for exploration, Hayle was gone before we got a proper look at it and our path took us through Lelant, along the River Hayle estuary, looking out to sea.

The pale-gold, sandy beaches were deserted and looked almost tropical, an effect somewhat marred by the grey skies and the occasional dog walker wrapped up in coat, scarf and hat. In the distance, to the north of us, the lighthouse could just be made out on Godrevy Island.

We followed the path which, in its turn, followed the railway line heading towards St Ives, pausing frequently to change clothing or to adjust rucksack straps, slowly remembering how to hike again after the long winter break.

St Ives was quiet and dull, the overcast sky reflected in the still sea and doubling the impression of greyness. Jeff and I made our way through the holiday flats and hotels, downhill towards the harbour. It was getting near to dinner-time and our plan was to find a pleasant pub and enjoy the evening with a meal before heading out of town and finding a suitable spot on

Howling at the Moon

which to camp.

We were spoilt for choice in the narrow streets around the harbour, but eventually we took our pick and found a place to eat. The pub was dark and warm and cosy, and I wondered how easy it would be to walk back out of it when the time came, and to sleep on a windy clifftop.

Night was falling as we left the pub, feeling pleasantly full and more than a little soporific. The cool outdoor air perked me up and I quickly realised that if we wanted to avoid walking along the clifftops in the coming darkness, we'd better get a move on.

The coast to the west of St Ives is covered in an ancient field system, small paddocks divided up by stone walls. Unfortunately for us, the fields were disused and densely packed with brambles, and it was over an hour and on the very cusp of nightfall by the time we found a field which was flat, grassed and not obviously visible from the coast path.

It was a still evening but, when it blows, the prevailing wind in the UK comes from the west, so we set up our tents facing east and began organising ourselves for the night. We were soon asleep.

*****

I was woken up early the next morning by bright sunshine. Breakfast and breaking camp convinced me that I could still snap into last year's routines and do the things that had to be done, and complete those tasks quickly and economically. Fed, relatively clean and with everything packed, I stood for a few minutes and watched the sunlight reflecting off the dappled surface of the sea, then wandered over to Jeff's tent to see how he was progressing.

Jeff was sitting in the entrance to his tent with his feet sticking out of it, finishing his breakfast by spooning food out of a foil packet and into his mouth.

I was in a conversational mood.

"What are you having?"

Jeff contemplated the back of his spoon, which had traces of food stuck to it, and then looked up at me.

"Lancashire hotpot."

"Bloody hell – you're a bit of a gourmet. I wouldn't fancy that for breakfast."

Jeff licked the spoon, folded the top of the foil pouch and put it into a plastic bag.

"It's all calories. It doesn't bother me."

We made an early start and the sun continued to rise as we walked. The only clouds in the sky formed a thin, scrappy-looking line just above the far horizon out to sea. Pale-blue sky and dark-blue sea presaged a beautiful day ahead. I hoped we'd get most of our walking done before the day got too hot.

There is a lot of in and out along this section of the coast path, and there's no escaping that fact if you wish to walk along the coast. The path follows closely against the cliff edge and seems to mirror almost every fluctuation in the line of the coast. To add variety, it also dips back down to sea level every time it crosses a brook, then climbs back up to clifftop height until it crosses the next one.

In my experience, many coastal paths in southern England have a second path or a road running almost parallel but slightly further inland. Let's face it, if you didn't need to look down into every bay and inlet like the coastguards of old did, why would you stick religiously to the line of the coast with its ins and outs, its ups and downs? If you were only taking a pig to market or courting that pretty lass on the next farm, you'd take the most direct route open to you. Jeff and I were on the coast path, though, and that's where we stayed. It might not have been the most direct route, but it was *our* route.

*****

Just past Pen Enys Point we found a stone circle.

Cornwall is littered with ancient remains, some dating back to the middle of the Stone Age about 20,000 years ago, some more recent. In bygone days, some landowners "restored" the old ruins on their land or even, to keep up with the fashion of the day, built their own ruins from scratch to impress their neighbours.

Jeff and I were standing in Treveal Stone Circle. It wasn't marked on my map, a fact which didn't help me work out whether it was an ancient monument or a rich man's garden ornament, or both.

Twelve stones stood in a circle about ten metres in diameter. The stones weren't large: about a metre or slightly less in height, with a thirteenth stone about a metre and a half tall standing at the southern end of the circle. Whatever their purpose might have been, their very presence and the fact that they'd probably stood here for thousands of years added to the feeling of emptiness and abandonment along this lonely coastline. A potent reminder, if one were needed, that we were on the fringes of the British Isles.

The morning got warmer as we walked on. To our right, the sea was calm and flat and blue; translucent, almost tropical-looking as we peered down into the tiny bays from our clifftop hike. To our left, Cornwall rose up, covered in brown bracken or dun-coloured grass. When we could see higher ground we caught glimpses of bright green fields, enclosed by stone walls.

Just before Zennor, Jeff told me his knees felt sore. He fancied a break, he said.

We took a breather on the clifftop and swigged water. I looked around us, at the small fields bordered by Cornish granite "hedges". The farming system here dates from the Bronze Age, about 4,000BCE in Cornwall.

I pulled my mind back to the present. My data sheet suggested a pub in Zennor, less than a kilometre from where we were standing. I proposed that we slip into the village to

The Dry Run

see what we could find, and the motion was quickly passed. There being no other business, the meeting concluded and the participants dispersed down the hill towards Zennor.

In Zennor we found a chapel which had been converted into a backpackers' hostel with, ideally for our purposes, a tearoom on the ground floor. We took a table outside in the sunshine and drank tea. I ate cake.

I noticed that Jeff wasn't eating.

"You off your nosebag?"

He looked at my cake.

"I could still do with losing a few pounds."

I shovelled in a mouthful of cake.

"This is not the time to be cutting back on the calories. You can do that at home, not when you're out here, walking long distances and carrying a pack."

Jeff was unimpressed.

"I'm still over the weight I was when I did Hadrian's Wall. This is a good opportunity to lose a bit more."

I pushed my plate away.

"Well, I intend to cram down all the calories I can, and they taste even better when I haven't had to carry them."

We paid our bill and walked back through Zennor village, towards the coast path. As we strolled along the lane, I wondered which house had been occupied by D.H. Lawrence and his German wife Frieda during their stay here.

The Lawrences had first met in Nottingham in 1912. He had just given up teaching to become a full-time writer, she was married with three young children. They fell in love, eloped to Germany and, in 1914, Frieda obtained a divorce so that they could marry.

From 1915 to 1917 the couple lived near Zennor. They were living on limited means and it wasn't a happy period for them. Accused of spying for the Germans and suspected of signalling to German submarines, they suffered constant harassment from the authorities. Maybe there was something about Lawrence, or maybe it was his British-German marriage. Maybe it was his in-laws (Frieda was a distant relative of Manfred von Richtofen, the flying ace known as the Red Baron). Whatever the reason, the episode culminated with the authorities making an order under the Defence of the Realm Act and the Lawrences were given three days' notice to leave the county of Cornwall. The irony cannot have been lost on Lawrence: during his elopement to Germany back in 1912 with Frieda, he had been arrested by the Germans as a suspected British spy.

Coincidentally, in July 1916, two ships sank off this stretch of coast, but neither sinking had anything to do with the Lawrences or with German submarines.

In 1916 the British Army was still largely horse-powered and the First World War was at its height. The steamer *Neto* was carrying feed for the Army's horses in France but ran aground in thick fog on Gurnard's Head, near Zennor. While the salvage teams were working on the *Neto,* the *Enrico Parodi*, a collier, ran aground close by, another casualty of the fog.

The *Neto* was wrecked but the *Enrico Parodi* looked as if she could be re-floated, so the salvage workers turned their attentions from the *Neto* to her. Unfortunately the bow of the *Enrico Parodi* split open as she was being towed and she sank next to The Carracks.

Jeff and I walked on under clear blue skies, next to a crystal blue sea, with a stiffening breeze in our faces. I occasionally checked our progress against my wristwatch and my map: the path wasn't too testing and we were making good time.

Very soon we reached the old engine-house for the Gurnard's Head Mine. The mine was known as the Treen Copper Mine when it was started, sometime before 1821, but by 1877 it was disused. Parts of the engine-house still stand next to the mineshaft, looking as they might topple into it at

The Dry Run

any moment. The wind and the sunshine created an impression of wildness and it was difficult to imagine the hive of human activity that this place must once have been.

Just past the old mine, still on Treen Cove, are the remains of an ancient church named Chapel Jane, and we paused to look at it. This chapel was mentioned in the Domesday Book of 1086 and the word "Jane" in the name is thought to derive from the Cornish word for "wild", rather than the name of a woman. The chapel was built into a hollow carved into the cliff at this lovely spot. The walls were still seven feet high during the mid-nineteenth century, but today they can only just be made out. A more modern altar has been added.

Prayers, however, were doing nothing for Jeff's knees and he was finding it more and more difficult to keep going along the ups and downs of the coast path. We stopped and I ate some chocolate while we discussed our options.

Jeff was obviously in some pain and although it was only mid-afternoon, it seemed wise to draw the day's walking to some sort of conclusion. We could carry on along the coast path, cut across the fields to the B road and walk along that, or we could rest here in the sunshine and, after a leisurely dinner, throw our tents up, out of sight behind a hedge.

I put the options to Jeff.

I thought he'd plump for the "camp here" scenario but he was adamant that he wanted to press on along the coast path. From what I could see, from the map and from the ground in front of me, the coastal path between here and Pendeen was more of the same. But we were under no pressure, I argued. Wouldn't he prefer to relax here, rest his legs and enjoy the good weather, and then camp in such a lovely spot?

No, he wouldn't, as it turned out. Forward progress was the name of the game. We were about 4km away from the pub in Pendeen - a pub which served food and kept a campsite. Jeff perked up when the pub was mentioned. We agreed to move up onto the B road, which should make for easier going, and follow it into Pendeen village. We'd camp and eat at the pub, then assess the state of Jeff's knees. Tomorrow would be, as they say, another day.

We crossed three or four fields and I got the distinct impression that things were getting worse in the knee department. The expression on Jeff's face was that of a man in pain and every time I turned around, he was a little further behind me.

I reached the B road and leaned on my walking poles next to an old stone barn while I waited for Jeff to catch up. At least, I reasoned, we would have flat, easy walking for the next hour to get to the pub.

Jeff rounded the barn. I tried to raise morale.

"Straight down this road. About an hour and we should be there."

I expected a rueful grin and a humorous, throwaway comment, but what I got was a grimace and a gruff, "Thank fuck for that." It didn't bode well.

We set off along the road.

Out in front, I did some thinking. I knew Jeff had walked before, but on this trip he'd lasted half a day. And we hadn't covered any great distance in that time. I wondered if he was nursing an injury he hadn't told me about.

I thought through alternatives to our planned walk along the coast path and realised that, because of the nature of this walk, we had an almost infinite number of options. We'd planned, in effect, to walk three quarters of what was roughly the circumference of an oval, from Hayle to Penzance. At any point on our walk we could, if we chose, simply turn and walk in a straight line across the oval, taking a shortcut to our destination. The beauty of this approach was that we could select a shortcut at almost any stage of our hike, and we could make that shortcut as long or as short as we liked. I'd tried to explain this to Jeff when we left the coast path but his response suggested that he hadn't understood. I decided to go over it again with him when we reached the pub. No matter what state he was in, there was a suitable walking option available.

Jeff was visibly limping now, and wincing as he walked. I paused to allow him to catch me up. He nodded towards a cluster of rooftops in the distance ahead of us.

"At least we haven't got far to go."

This surprised me. I was sure I'd told him that we had an hour of walking ahead of us, and that couldn't have been more than five minutes ago.

"That's not it, mate. That's not even halfway."

"What! For fuck's sake!"

"I don't mind camping there, if you want to stop. But if you want the pub and a shower, it's a bit further than those houses."

He didn't want to stop there, but I got the distinct impression he didn't want to go on either. I thought I'd let him choose.

"You tell me what you want and we'll do that."

As I said it, I hoped he wouldn't say that he wanted a pub right here, because there wasn't one.

Jeff decided to keep going.

After about an hour of struggle we arrived at the pub in Pendeen. At the back of the pub was a large field with a few caravans lined up at the end of the field nearest the pub buildings. The wind was strengthening. Jeff took off his rucksack and put it down on the grass.

"You've broken me."

I looked at him, surprised. It hadn't been my decision to keep walking.

"Let's get the tents up and see about some dinner in the pub."

Jeff looked at his rucksack, lying forlornly on its side on the ground.

"I'm not sleeping in the bloody dirt again."

The emphasis in his voice surprised me, and he sounded as if he'd made his mind up.

"Where are you going to sleep then?"

"In the pub. I'm going to ask if they do B&B."

So we walked into the pub, enquired about bed and breakfast, learned the prices and walked straight back out again.

Five minutes had elapsed and there we were, back on the same spot in the camping field, next to Jeff's rucksack.

The wind was still picking up and I could see that some sort of shelter from it would help us through the night. I put that thought to Jeff.

"It might be worth pitching the tents in the lee of those caravans, to keep the wind off us in the night."

"I don't like the sound of that. The people in them might nick our stuff."

"I don't think they will. And I didn't bring any valuables. If they nick my stuff, all they're going to get is practice."

I've found that people tend to respond better to someone with whom they've had some sort of interaction, so I wandered over to a lady with blonde hair and a black fleece who was emerging from the door of one of the caravans.

"We're looking to put a couple of small tents out of the wind for the night. Will we be in anyone's way if we camp along here?"

She tapped a propane gas bottle as if testing how full it was.

"You can put them right next to my place if you want. That'll be out of the wind. And next door are away so they won't bother."

I thanked her. She nodded towards Jeff.

"What's up with your mate?"

"He's in pain. His knees are playing him up."

She sniffed.

The Dry Run

"Tell him to man up. This is Cornwall."

I wandered back to Jeff, wondering as I did so what his reaction would be if I told him the woman had no interest in his stuff but that she thought he should man up because this was Cornwall. On balance, I decided against it.

"She's all right. She said we can camp near the caravans, out of the wind."

Jeff shouldered his rucksack.

"I'm not sleeping next to that lot", and he walked to the middle of the field and began setting up his tent.

I set up camp near the caravans and made myself a cup of tea. I didn't like where this was going: what should have been a few days gentle walking was becoming distinctly problematic. I was starting to get doubts about the Pennine Way, but I pushed them out of my mind. After all, this was surely what a dry run was all about? Identify problems and sort them out before the main event. But a little voice kept telling me that the main event might be one man light. And I wasn't sure how I felt about that.

Dinner in the pub was a subdued affair. Jeff seemed more himself, but told me he'd be leaving in the morning.

I pointed out that we had a variety of routes we could choose from. We could walk the planned 25km each day, or take shorter days. We could walk just a few kilometres each day if we wished to, and then relax in the sunshine. But every option I outlined drew the same response from Jeff: a minicab to Penzance Station and the train home. The best I could get was an agreement to "sleep on it" and make a decision in the morning, although I suspected the decision was already made.

Later that evening, as I wriggled down into my sleeping bag, I realised that I had a decision to make too. In the immortal words of Joe Strummer, should I stay or should I go?

Yesterday, in one of my lighter moments, I'd joked about leaving Jeff behind and strongly advised him to keep the last bullet for himself, but I knew I'd feel bad about leaving

41

him, especially with an injury. But this wasn't all about how I felt. How would Jeff feel, I pondered? He might, of course, be glad to see the back of me.

I didn't want to come all this way and then cut the walk short, but I didn't want to abandon a mate either. I decided I'd ask him in the morning. If he needed help to get home, I'd go with him. If he didn't, I'd wish him well and press on.

*****

Next morning, I woke up with the dawn and enjoyed a leisurely breakfast while still in my sleeping bag. The sky was overcast, but the grey clouds looked very high up. The wind had dropped a little since yesterday evening. It might be a nice day, I decided, or it might not.

I pulled on my trail shoes and stood outside my tent on the dewy grass while I cleaned my teeth. Across the field, Jeff's tent looked as if it had been hit by a hurricane. It sagged more than a tent should sag and bits of it flapped haphazardly in the wind. I wondered if he was awake yet. Given his feelings yesterday, I thought it unlikely that he would be having a lie-in.

I put my toothbrush away and walked across the camping field. The door of Jeff's tent was open and as I got closer I could see his legs and feet sticking out. I gave him a cheery, "Morning!", and he wriggled around so that I could see his face and he could see me.

"How you feeling?"

When he answered, his manner was upbeat but his words weren't:

"I'm OK, but my knees are gone."

I wanted, really wanted, to ask, if his knees were gone, what was connecting his arse to his feet? But I know that my sense of humour isn't to everyone's taste, so I discarded that thought almost as soon as I had it.

The Dry Run

"What happened to your tent?"

Jeff grimaced.

"Bloody thing blew down twice in the night. First time I got out and put it up again, went round and put all the pegs back in. The second time I thought, fuck it, and went back to sleep with the wet tent flapping about on top of me. I tell you, I really have had enough of this lark."

This didn't sound good. I wondered if I might be able to move his mind from camping to walking, so I tried to take us back to our conversation last night in the pub.

"Do you fancy one of the shorter routes? We could go slowly, do a short distance and camp?"

"No, mate. I've had enough. I'm going home."

That thought brought me down with a bump.

"OK. I'll come with you to give you a hand. Do you want me to take some of your stuff?"

Jeff was instantly gracious.

"There's no need for you to come. It's a nice offer, but I don't want to spoil your walk. I can get myself home all right."

I knew they had a list of minicab telephone numbers in the pub because we'd mentioned it the night before.

"Minicab to Penzance and train home?"

"Yeah. Where is the nearest station? Is it a long way?"

I could answer that one without looking at my map.

"It's five miles to Penzance from here."

"Is that all? I thought it was much further."

"That's what the road sign in the village said."

I thought I'd give it one last shot.

"We could walk five miles, couldn't we? We've got all day."

Jeff was adamant.

"I'm done in. I'm going home and then I'm going to the doctor."

I couldn't argue with that, so I returned to my tent and

43

took it down. Ten minutes later I was back at Jeff's tent, but his plan was unchanged. I shouldered my rucksack, said my goodbyes and set off once more.

It was a strange feeling as I paced down the main street of the village in the early morning. The last few hours of walking the day before had been almost painful, I felt, and I wasn't the one with the injury. It wasn't that I was nervous about walking alone: I've walked many long-distance paths unaccompanied and I knew I could set a better pace on my own. My sticking point was that I hadn't planned to hike solo. I'd planned to have, and to enjoy, company on this trip.

I wondered if Jeff would be fit for the Pennine Way. I thought he probably might, since it was his idea in the first place; as if we can simply wish ourselves fit for something that we very much want to do.

I caught a glimpse of the old Geevor tin mine over to my right and I remembered reading somewhere that some of these old tin and copper mines extend out from the land as far as 2,000 feet under the sea. I paused and thought about that for a few seconds. I wondered if I could even see 2,000 feet out to sea.

Geevor was the last-but-one mine in Cornwall when it finally closed in 1990, and since then the last remaining mine has shut too. Thousands of years of activity and expertise, now all gone.

That was a further depressing thought, so I pushed it out of my mind and hiked on through St Just, lost in contemplation. Soon, I found myself at Land's End.

Crass and commercialised it might be, but Land's End was selling coffee and I was in the mood for one. I was the only customer that early, "before the coaches arrive" as the waitress put it, and the whole place was very quiet. I drank my coffee, then ordered another and took some solid calories on board for good measure. A few photographs and a look at the views, and then it was time to leave the north Cornish coast path and set out along the south Cornish coast path. I had turned towards my journey's end: the town of Penzance.

I strode around the coastline, buoyed up by the fact that I was making good time and was well ahead of my schedule. The sun emerged and got stronger and stronger, so much so that I could feel it burning me and I had to stop and dig my sun hat out of my pack. My next problem was keeping the hat on my head as the strong breeze stiffened into a gale.

I enjoyed the easy walking along gravel tracks and paths, around the undulating, short-grassed cliffs, with the wind roaring and battering at me, and the waves crashing on the rocks below.

Soon, Gwennap Head showed me its day marks for shipping, looming large and unexplained, like something left over from a 1960s sci-fi television series. The seaward mark is a large, red cone, with the landward mark a black and white pepper-pot shape some distance behind it, both of them looking totally out of place amongst the rough gorse bushes. The marks were erected by Trinity House in 1821 to warn shipping of the Runnel Stone, a mile offshore. If you're out on the water and you can see the red cone *and* the black and white marker, then all's well. If you can see the red marker but *not* the black and white marker (because it's obscured by the red marker as you look), then you are right over the Runnel Stone and in danger. There's also a buoy directly over the stone so, as ship's master, you really have no excuse.

Despite that, between 1880 and 1923 over thirty ships ran foul of the Runnel Stone. The situation was eased somewhat in 1923 when the *SS City of Westminster* hit the reef with such force that the top layer of stone was torn away. Seventy-two people were saved from the ship and no vessel has hit the Runnel Stone since. I guess maybe there isn't enough left to be a hazard after the 1923 incident. The *City of Westminster*, incidentally, was not recovered and is still there.

Lunchtime saw me in Porthgwarra, a strange, quirky

little village where the route from the houses to the beach is a tunnel through the cliff. The tunnel was dug by tin miners to give local farmers a horse-and-cart route to and from the beach, so that they could collect seaweed for fertiliser. A second tunnel contains man-made tidal pools where live shellfish could be stored ready to be taken to market.

I passed a rectangular ruin with a spring in it, and a convenient noticeboard informed me that this was a holy place: St Levan's Well. The well and the remains of the chapel a bit further down the slope are believed to date from the seventh or eighth century.

I had time in hand, and it was a lovely spot at which to have lingered, but I had a taste for forward progress and I pressed on.

I rounded the headland, passed the open-air Minack Theatre, and descended into Porthcurno below it.

The little village of Porthcurno rose from obscurity in 1870, when the first underwater telegraph cable came ashore here. Falmouth was the more obvious choice, but Falmouth was a busy port with the risk of damage to the cables caused by ships' anchors, so the much quieter Porthcurno was chosen.

The cable linked Porthcurno with Lisbon, which was already linked to Bombay in India, one of the most prized possessions in the British Empire. A line to London was established and Porthcurno became the British terminal of the Empire's telegraphic network. The original concrete hut still stands near the beach.

Just two years later, the Eastern Telegraph Company was formed and Porthcurno became its training centre. Staff trained at this little outpost in deepest Cornwall were posted all over the world.

In 1928, the Eastern Telegraph Company merged with Marconi's Wireless Telegraph Company to become Imperial and International Communications Ltd, and in 1934 the merged company became Cable and Wireless. The site was so important that in 1940, mining engineers dug a secret tunnel into the cliff face to protect the telegraph equipment from attack by the Germans.

The cable office closed in 1970 but the training college kept going until 1993, when it also closed and was converted into holiday flats. Porthcurno is far from dormant, however, and six new high-capacity fibre-optic cables now run up the beach.

Every beach along this part of the coast necessitates a steep descent to reach it and a push uphill to gain the next headland after it, so I didn't want to dally because I knew I had a sharp uphill ahead of me. I left Porthcurno and hiked on up the coast path.

I knew there were several campsites in the area and I fancied a night of semi-civilised indulgence, by which I mean a flush toilet and a cold water tap, so I tried the first of them. It was a wind-blasted field and, try as I might, I couldn't find a spot sufficiently sheltered for me to camp overnight.

The second campsite was even worse and I got the impression that neither site had ever been planned for backpackers. It seemed as if the farmers had decided there was money to be made by diversifying, so they had done no more then take a convenient field and call it a campsite. Some little provision had been made for motor home and caravan users, but none at all for hikers.

It had been a long day, but sometimes circumstances dictate that you keep walking. I could have wild camped. It would have been easy to fill my water bottles at either of these two campsites, find a grassy field out of the wind and pitch my tent for the night, but I knew that there was still another site a little further along the coast. I could water-up there and go on if necessary.

I soon passed a large, chambered Stone Age tomb, and then arrived at the Merry Maidens Stone Circle.

This stone circle stands in a field. It's about twenty-four

metres in diameter and it comprises nineteen granite megaliths. It dates from the late Neolithic, about 3,000 to 2,000BCE. The stones are around one and a half metres high.

The story is that nineteen maidens were turned to stone (presumably by God) as punishment for dancing on the Sabbath. The two large stones a little distance away from the circle are said to be the pipers who played for them, also petrified. Many old stone circles have a legend about people being turned to stone and my suspicion is that these stories were started by the early Christian priests, to break any links with the old, pre-Christian religions and to deter any backsliding into Paganism on the part of their flock.

The third campsite I called at was empty and I wondered if it was still trading. What I took to be the camping field looked unmown and disused. Nearby, a Victorian farmhouse was guarded by a gang of about twenty mangy-looking cats. The doorstep, the walls around the front garden, the path, the windowsills, just about every flat surface had one or more dirty cats on it and they all looked down on me or up at me with utter contempt. I don't know if you've ever walked through a rough estate and been scrutinised thoroughly by the local youths while doing so, but that was the impression the cats created. I wondered what sort of nutcase would keep so many cats and in such poor condition.

In an effort to be friendly, I tweeted the nearest one and tried a, "Hello, puss." The cat ignored me, got up languidly, turned its back on me and walked slowly down the path with its tail in the air and its arse pointing at me. I considered giving it a nudge with my shoe for its cheek, but I couldn't see through the net curtains of the house and for all I knew I might be being watched. I still needed a campsite and I thought it best not to offend any cat lovers who might be within.

Bored with me, the remaining cats went back to studying each other.

I knocked at the door.

The Dry Run

After a few seconds it was answered by a man. I asked if I might camp. He looked surprised.

"Yeah." A pause. He appeared thoughtful. "Yeah. We're not really set up for the season yet. But you're welcome to camp if you like. As long as you don't mind using the Ladies, 'cause the water's off in the Gents."

I told him that would be fine and asked how much I owed him. He looked surprised.

"Oh no, I won't charge. We're not set up for the season yet."

The place didn't look as if it had been "set up for the season" for a few seasons, but I couldn't fault his kindness. I wandered around and around the field behind the farmhouse, trying to find a spot out of the wind but reasonably close to the water supply in the Ladies. I picked a spot close enough to the derelict barn for it to act as a windbreak, but far enough away to put any rats that might attempt the journey to my tent at great risk of being picked off by the army of cats.

*****

I spent a comfortable night and I was up early the next morning, and soon reached nearby Lamorna Cove. I paused before walking down the wooded valley. The last time I had been here had been on holiday with my parents as a small child, many, many years ago.

I passed a watermill, long-stilled. The legend on its cast-iron waterwheel informed me that it was made by Isaac Willey of Helston in 1907. It was last operational in 1919, the end of a milling tradition on this site that stretched back to the 1300s.

Like most of Cornwall, mineral extraction took place in Lamorna for almost as long as humans have lived there. Tin was taken from the stream from at least the 1300s, and granite was quarried on one side of the cove. It must have been good stuff, because Lamorna granite was used to build the Thames

Embankment, County Hall in London and the Admiralty Pier at Dover.

An uphill pull through drizzle under dark skies saw me to Mousehole and I paused by the harbour to admire the mercury barometer, set behind glass in a wall next to the harbour. A plaque next to it tells its story:

THE FITZROY BAROMETER

This barometer was originally loaned to Mousehole in 1854 by Admiral Fitzroy, founder of the Meteorological Office.

Its purpose was to provide data to the Met Office to improve storm warnings but also give the fishermen of the village warning of pending bad weather in an attempt to reduce the loss of life so common at the time

As I walked out of Mousehole, I passed a garden and a noticeboard that jogged my memory and made me a little ashamed that I hadn't remembered of my own accord. On 19th December 1981, the lifeboat from this little village (the *Solomon Brown*) was launched by its volunteer crew to go to the aid of a stricken ship, the *Union Star*. The lifeboat crew reported to the Coastguard by radio that they had saved four crew from the *Union Star*, but after that there was no further contact. There were no survivors from either vessel. Sixteen people died that night, eight from the *Solomon Brown* and eight from the *Union Star*. In such a small community everyone would have known someone who died or someone who was bereaved as a result. It's sobering to realise that, despite that knowledge and just two days after the tragedy, another eight people from Mousehole stepped forward to fill the lifeboat crew vacancies.

I walked on, through what looked like a post-industrial landscape to the fishing port of Newlyn, past the fish sheds,

The Dry Run

along a cold, windy promenade and into Penzance.

The dry run was done and I had plenty to think about on the train home.

*****

SMS message: 23/04, 09:35
From: Jeff

Hi John, hope you got back OK. I may have slightly torn my anterior ligament (think that's what she said) complicated by twisting (hence the bleed (lump) at the back and numbness). Been forwarded to hospital for a scan to check for anything else. No real treatment other than rest but I can still exercise moderately to keep it mobile and allow clots to break down. Can't run which is a pain in the arse. Pennine Way is out for me this year, I'm afraid.

*****

Chapter 3

Committed

*****

SMS message: 03/05, 17:18
From: John

I'm starting the Pennine Way tomorrow. Wish me luck.

*****

SMS message: 03/05, 17:22
From: Jeff

Doing it on your own? Best of luck – you should have great weather.

*****

SMS message: 03/05, 17:24
From: John

Yes, on my tod. Don't know about the weather. Forecast is chilly at night, so I'm taking a nice warm sleeping bag.

*****

SMS message: 03/05, 17:26
From: Jeff

Jealous! Really hope it goes well. Take care and keep me updated.

*****

Chapter 4

The Peak District

Alone at Edale. – Civil disobedience. – Over Exposed! – I meet Mike. – Britain's Appalachian Trail.

*****

Real life: Edale, 04/05, 15:40

*****

All of which is how I came to be standing alone at Edale railway station at twenty to four on a cold, sunny afternoon in May.

I was in Edale because the Pennine Way starts here.

The Pennine Way is classified as a National Trail and, maybe because it was Britain's first long-distance path, it's probably also the most well-known. Mention to anyone in the UK that you like walking and, even if they only walk as far as the pub, they'll ask you if you've walked the Pennine Way. It's the yardstick by which all serious walkers are measured.

I put my rucksack on a bench on the station platform and adjusted my trekking poles for walking. The small local train which had delivered me there pulled noisily out of the station and silence fell.

The Peak District

The only other passenger who had alighted pushed her pedal cycle along the platform and disappeared from view.

I sat down and put on my gaiters then stood up, I hoped with a purposeful air about me. I made my way out of the station and turned to walk up the lane towards the official start point of the Pennine Way, outside The Old Nag's Head pub.

The road was empty and there was no sign of life from the pub or the nearby cottages. Outside the pub, a painted wooden sign announced simply, "PENNINE WAY", with an arrow in case of doubt. A few paces further on, a metal sign riveted to a stone stated:

THE OFFICIAL START

OF THE

PENNINE WAY
KIRK YETHOLM 268 MILES / 429 KM

It all seemed a very underwhelming start to such a momentous undertaking.

Something didn't seem quite right about the metal plaque, so I checked my notes. On my maps, I'd measured the Pennine Way as being 423km long, or 263 miles, and that's the distance quoted by most maps and guidebooks. I know there's some vagueness about the length of most long-distance paths, usually because of route changes over the years interspersed with occasional squabbles about rights of way, but that plaque still didn't seem right. I did a quick calculation and found the 268 miles on the metal sign should, in any case, equal 431km, not the 429km stated.

Like any walker, when in doubt I always claim the longest distance, on the basis that it's more likely to impress friends and family, so 431km it was. It also occurred to me that the numbers suggested this walk was increasing in length as I was standing there doing mental arithmetic. The best thing would be to start walking the Pennine Way before it got any longer. With the trite thought that a journey of a thousand miles begins with a single step, I pushed the gate open and started up the path.

I walked up a well-trodden path next to a small stream. To each side of me, and overhead, tree branches arched up, still completely bare from the winter but substantial enough to block out the sunshine.

I stepped out of the tunnel of bare branches and walked across sheep pastures, through the bleating of new lambs, and threaded my way between day walkers coming off the moor and making their way back to Edale.

My path turned to follow the old stone steps of Jacob's Ladder up onto the moor and immediately I could see numerous snow patches lingering higher up, the last remnants of an unseasonal snowfall just the week before. The presence of snow added to my feeling of isolation.

I stopped for water at the Kinder Downfall and paused for a few minutes to look west, towards Hayfield. I was looking at the scene of the Kinder Trespass, a mass act of civil disobedience which opened up the English countryside for all of us to enjoy. It was a poignant moment because, if those people hadn't stepped forward and made their point, I wouldn't have been here on Kinder eighty-four years later.

The Trespass took place on 24th April 1932 and was planned to draw attention to the fact that walkers were denied access to great tracts of countryside, in this case by landowners and gamekeepers, who preserved the land for seasonal grouse shooting, and by water board bailiffs. There were violent scuffles during the Trespass and six people were arrested.

With the exception of certain sensitive sites, such as diplomatic premises, railways, nuclear installations and the like, trespass is not a criminal offence in England and so the six were charged with offences relating to violence towards the keepers. One of the organisers of the Trespass was Benny

The Peak District

Rothman of the Young Communist League of Manchester and the involvement of communists was guaranteed to perturb Middle-England. Prison sentences of between two and six months were handed down.

Despite this setback, a fuse had been lit. The Ramblers' Association took up the cause and campaigned until the Countryside and Rights of Way Act established rights to walk on "access land" in 2000, some 68 years later. Supporters argue that the Kinder Trespass was the most successful act of civil disobedience in British history, pointing to the Act of 2000, the establishment of long-distance footpaths and the National Parks legislation, the latter passed in 1949.

And history seems to bear out the Kinder Trespassers: the Peak District National Park is one of the most visited national parks in the UK and attracts over ten million visitors each year.

I strode on across the Kinder Plateau and down the other side, taking a sharp right at Mill Hill and following a ridge of high ground towards an A road, far in the distance. The sun was getting low and I'd had a busy day, so I was looking for somewhere to camp. My problem was that flat bits of ground big enough to put a tent on were few and far between, and those I could find were under two or three inches of water. If the higher ground was like that, I reasoned, there was no point in looking further down the slope.

I pressed on, feeling as if I was racing the sunset, and eventually found a patch that was almost flat and not as boggy as its surroundings. It was a compromise, I felt, but sometimes compromise is necessary, and I put the tent up.

I was at a crossroads, where the old Roman road known as Doctor's Gate intersects the Pennine Way. I prepared my dinner and sorted through my kit inside my tent. It looked like a chilly night was in the offing, but I was quietly confident. I'd covered a reasonable distance given my late start from Edale, I had a reasonable site on which to camp and I was sure I'd be warm and comfortable through the night.

I'm not troubled by ghosts, mainly because I don't believe in them. At least, no-one who does believe has ever been able to offer me any evidence that they exist. And that was just as well, because I was sleeping in an area littered with aircraft crash sites.

Five minutes' walk to the north of me was the wreckage of a USAF Boeing RB29 Superfortress, a huge aircraft that crashed here in 1948. The Superfortress carried the name *Over Exposed!* because she had been deployed to photograph the atomic bomb tests at Bikini Atoll in the Pacific and had got too close to the flash. All 13 crew were lost here on Bleaklow, killed just three days before they were due to return to the USA after surviving the Second World War.

The remains of a Douglas Dakota can be found a short walk away and, just past that, the resting place of a Lancaster bomber.

Like I said, it's a good thing I'm not troubled by ghosts.

*****

The next day dawned bright and clear. It was cold that early in the morning and I was glad I'd brought a warm sleeping bag. I looked back the way I'd come and gave a silent vote of thanks to whoever had decided to lay the flagstones that formed the path up here. I knew the stones were put down to reduce erosion, but they're a great help to walkers because this area would be a long, dirty swamp-walk without them.

I made an early start, setting off along the path up Bleaklow Head, feeling cheerful in the sunshine. I soon started to sweat and when the paved sections ran out I quickly noticed how rough the terrain was. I stuck to the southern edge of the deep, steep-sided Torside Clough, pushing my way through the heather, knee-high but still dormant from winter, and before long I found myself looking down on the deep blue of Torside

The Peak District

Reservoir directly ahead of me but still in the distance.

Maybe it was the warm morning, maybe it was taking me a while to get back into the swing of hiking, but I was feeling the strain. My pack felt heavy and my legs felt slow. I forgot how warm and cosy I'd been last night and mentally cursed myself for bringing the heavier sleeping bag. "Of mankind we may say in general they are fickle."[1]

On Blackchew Head the uphill stretches seemed to come relentlessly, one after another. I paused to take water from a small stream and stood there for a few seconds, enjoying the taste and the feel of the cold water.

Next was a long stretch, thankfully paved with large flagstones, up Soldier's Lump and Black Hill. The stones underfoot were all different sizes which made it impossible to get into a walking rhythm, but the alternative was deep peat bog and that didn't bear thinking about.

Wessenden Moor was every shade of khaki, the grass rippling gently in the breeze. It must have looked very different during the Industrial Revolution, I reflected, when this area was known as The Black Moor because it was covered in soot from the local mills and factories.

My reverie was interrupted by the next twist in the Pennine Way. I'd been strolling along a pleasant gravel track which followed the contours above Wessenden Reservoir. A signpost pointed me ninety degrees to my left, away from my easy track, straight down the precipitous valley side to the stream at the bottom and then straight back up the other side, which looked even steeper and even higher.

There was no chance of me losing the path, I reflected as I puffed up the opposite side. The ground was so steep that the Pennine Way was right in front of my nose.

I topped out and followed an obvious path between

---

[1] *Niccolo Machiavelli (1469-1527).*

Swellands and Black Moss Reservoirs. It was a peaceful scene around me, albeit pretty bleak, and it belied the disaster which occurred during its construction. These two reservoirs were built by the Huddersfield Canal Company to feed their canal, and while Swellands Reservoir was being built in November 1810, the dam burst. The resulting surge of water drowned six people further down the valley, five of them from one family.

The sky had clouded over and the moor stayed bleak as I left Black Moss and Swellands behind me. In the distance I could see yet another reservoir, an incongruous patch of grey in the dull light-brown of the moor. Next to it was a building which, if my calculations were correct, should be The Carriage House, a pub which has many outstanding attributes, two of which particularly appealed to me: it allowed camping and it served food.

There were two tents already on the camping field when I arrived, and an older chap with a goatee beard who was putting up a third. I quickly chose my spot and put up my tent, then wandered round to size up my fellow campers. They comprised Judith, who had chosen the Pennine Way for her first long-distance hike; Mike, with the goatee, and Nigel who, as fortune would have it, lived just a few miles from me in Essex.

Judith was tending her blisters, not a good sign on Day Two of a long walk. Nigel had just finished putting up a large four-person tent. He'd provided himself with living quarters that were solid in construction and almost palatial in size, but which would also constitute a very heavy load on his back for every pace of his journey.

The next morning I was up at 5.15 and walking again by 7 o'clock. As I hiked the half mile back along the road to reach the Pennine Way, I wondered what the hell I'd been doing for nearly two hours. Maybe I wasn't as slick or as organised as I thought I was. I certainly should be able to get breakfast and strike camp in under an hour. One to watch tomorrow, I decided.

I passed an old engine-house almost opposite the pub campsite and, when I turned, I could see the brick air vents up on the hillside behind me. I knew that the four Standedge Tunnels run under this site, one canal tunnel and three rail tunnels. The engine-house used to house a steam engine and it was left over from the construction of the tunnel for the Huddersfield Narrow Canal between 1795 and 1811. The remains of it still sit on the moor surrounded by heaps of spoil dug out from the tunnel. At over 5km, the tunnel is the longest and highest canal tunnel in the UK and it was used extensively by the engineers and labourers who built the railway tunnels which parallel it. I couldn't work out whether the air vents related to the canal tunnel or the railway tunnels, or both.

It took me about ten minutes to re-join the Pennine Way and I turned onto it, heading north once more. My journey had only just started, but north was already beginning to feel like my default setting and there was a vague feeling of comfort which went with that.

The Pennine Way was the invention of Tom Stephenson, a journalist and walker. Stephenson was inspired by the creation of the Appalachian Trail in the USA and proposed a British long-distance trail in 1935. He even lobbied Parliament on one occasion.

The Way was originally planned to end at Wooler in Northumberland but it was decided that Kirk Yetholm, just the other side of the border fence in Scotland, would be a more fitting finishing point. The trail opened completely in 1965, proving just how long it can take for a good idea to become accepted in this country.

The Pennine Way has long been popular with walkers and it's been estimated that around 12,000 long-distance hikers complete it annually. I found that figure quite staggering when I read it. If we do the maths, on average 33 people complete the Pennine Way *every day.* I stopped and looked around me, but I couldn't see another walker. Not one. Where were they all?

I passed a stone which informed me that I had just walked past

> THE MOST
> EASTERLY POINT
> IN THE
> COUNTY OF
> LANCASHIRE

although precisely why that fact was worthy of note I couldn't fathom. Have the good folk of Lancashire also marked the most northerly, southerly and westerly points of their fair county? I didn't know. Good luck to them, I decided, if they have. Nothing wrong with a little community pride, and if there was a bit more of it about maybe some places might be a shade less depressing to live in and to pass through.

Or could it be because that spot on the map is now, and has been since 1974, part of Greater Manchester? Might someone be making a point?

I didn't know. The moors didn't look like my mental picture of Manchester, but that probably says more about me than it does about Manchester.

Chapter 5

The South Pennines

Walking the reservoirs. – May's Aladdin's Cave. – Inspiration of the Brontë sisters. – Simple pleasures, hard won. – Lynmouth in Lothersdale.

My path followed the contours for a while, and I enjoyed the easy walking and the views out across the lower ground. I like a bit of history served with my walks, but I was getting bored with reservoirs. These weren't the bucolic, tree-lined water features that enhance lowland England: up here, each reservoir seemed to be no more than a functional, pewter-grey slab, set in the dun-coloured moorland. No-nonsense northern reservoirs, solidly-built in the early nineteenth century to supply drinking water to the burgeoning industrial towns and to fill the canals which connected them. I checked my route on the map and then counted the reservoirs on just one fold of it: twenty-four. I could increase that number even further simply by folding the map out a little more.

I caught up with Mike, who had been one of my fellow campers at The Carriage House last night, and together we reached a burger van by the side of an A road just before the Pennine Way crosses the M62 motorway. A good spot, and a good time, for tea.

We stirred milk into our drinks at the counter which ran

along the side of the burger van, then made our way over to a flat rock which would serve as a seat and went through the cautious pleasantries and exploratory probes that people do in these situations.

I discovered that Mike was a well-experienced long-distance walker. A member of the Long Distance Walkers Association, he had walked many of the longer trails in the UK and had taken part in many "challenge" events, walking and navigating long distances against the clock. He was also, as I found out gradually over the next few days, good company.

We finished our drinks and squashed our paper cups. As we stood up it was impossible to avoid noticing that we were surrounded by discarded cups, empty bottles and burger cartons. We seemed to be at the centre of a litter explosion, most of which seemed to have originated from the burger van. It spread out in all directions and declined in volume as distance from our position increased, a similar concept to the spread of radiation after a nuclear explosion. We'd been taking tea at a sort of garbage ground zero.

I asked for Mike's cup and dutifully took our empties back to the van, dropping them into the black bin liner by the rear door of it. The motorway was a soft, persistent hum in the background.

We left the litter fallout zone and crossed the M62 together, then drifted apart along Blackstone Edge because we walked at different speeds. I passed the Aiggin Stone, a 600 year old waymark for travellers, and dropped down to the next road.

The White House pub might have been a good location to chat some more with Mike, but it was closed at that time of the morning and Mike was by now a small figure beneath a big rucksack, back in the distance behind me. I turned onto the water board track across Chelburn Moor and lost sight of him altogether.

A helpful schematic on a signboard reminded me that the

The South Pennines

Pennine Way was 268 miles long and showed clearly that I had walked very little of it. Navigation was as easy as it gets along this stretch and that left me with spare mental capacity, so I used that capacity to think.

I thought about the dry run in Cornwall, about walking without Jeff and about how much I'd enjoyed the simple pleasure of chatting with Mike at the burger van before the M62. Lightweight backpacking often reminds me of the importance of basic human needs: warmth, shelter, food, human contact.

I paused to read another noticeboard which told me about a conservation project, and that 96% of the land cover here was blanket bog. I hoped my path would take me over the remaining 4%.

The sunshine was weak and hazy, and there was a cold edge to the wind. In the distance, I could see the obelisk on Stoodley Pike and I knew I'd pass it within the hour. A low wall along the edge of Warland Drain offered a convenient seat, so I pulled out my woolly hat to keep warm and stopped for lunch.

I'd gone through the boring-tuna-and-plain-biscuit-course and was contemplating the much-more-interesting-chocolate-course when Mike rounded the bend in the path and asked if he could join me.

Mike kicked off his boots to air his feet and ate his lunch sitting next to me. He'd been wearing big, heavy traditional leather boots which dwarfed my light trail shoes. His actions reminded me that, on a long walk, you can never take too much care of your feet, so I followed his example and took my shoes off too. It's a simple, easy way to restore feet by ensuring that they're dry of sweat, but despite my good intentions, I rarely seem to get around to doing it. Maybe it's because the weather in the UK is seldom good enough to provide the benefit. If you take your shoes off here, the likelihood is that your feet will get wetter, not dryer. Or maybe it's that I'm lazy: if it's an action

65

that I can't take every day it doesn't become a habit and I don't do it. It was clearly a matter of routine to Mike.

We finished eating and put our rejuvenated feet back into our boots (Mike) and shoes (me), then set off across the moor again.

We soon reached Stoodley Pike Monument. It stands in a commanding position up on the hill and the inscription above the doorway into it tells its story:

STOODLEY PIKE
A BEACON MONUMENT
ERECTED BY PUBLIC SUBSCRIPTION
COMMENCED IN 1814 TO COMMEMORATE
THE SURRENDER OF PARIS TO THE ALLIES
AND FINISHED AFTER THE BATTLE OF
WATERLOO WHEN PEACE WAS ESTABLIS
HED IN 1815. BY A STRANGE COINCIDENCE
THE PIKE FELL ON THE DAY THE RUSSIAN
AMBASSADOR LEFT LONDON BEFORE THE
DECLARATION OF WAR WITH RUSSIA IN 1854.
WAS REBUILT WHEN PEACE WAS RESTORED IN
1856

To add a contemporary note, some anonymous sporting enthusiast had added the words, "Man City" in blue paint on one side of it.

*****

Just after Stoodley Pike, we split. Mike went on to camp at Colden and I dropped down into the town of Hebden Bridge to re-supply at the Co-op.

The lane which led down into Hebden Bridge was steep and narrow, and I paused for a while to lean on my poles and survey the little town beneath me. It had certainly changed since John Hillaby passed through in 1968 on his epic walk from Land's End to John O'Groats. Hillaby described rivers coloured by industrial pollutants, factories which "stand on each other's shoulders. They cling to the hillside. They are tucked away in yards and alleys; some are perched on the most improbable promontories." In Hillaby's day, Hebden was still an industrial town, a busy textile centre.

Hebden Bridge today looks a very different kettle of fish. It nestles between steep, wooded slopes, the trees still bare at the time I visited, the factories of Hillaby's time nowhere in evidence. The river appears clean enough and the factories and mill buildings that still survive were long ago turned into flats. In the 1970s Hebden's industry closed down and the town declined. Today it has a bohemian feel to it, a result of the creative and New Age people it attracts.

Dropping right down to the valley bottom to buy groceries at the Hebden Bridge Co-op left me with a steep climb back up through the village of Heptonstall to get to High Gate Farm, where Mike and I had planned to camp. Luckily, on the way there, I encountered a row of houses called *Slack Bottom*. My sense of humour is such that this find necessitated a rest break to take pictures.

High Gate Farm was attractive to Mike and I for a number of good reasons. Firstly, Pennine Way walkers can camp there for free. As if that wasn't enough, the place is close to the New Delight Inn which serves good food, good beer and has a very convivial landlord. Lastly, High Gate Farm contained May's Aladdin's Cave, a shop where you can buy almost anything at almost any time.

Mike was sitting at a table outside the shop finishing a cup of tea as I arrived. The shop lady asked us what time we planned to leave the next morning. We looked at each other and shrugged.

"We'll probably aim to leave about five-ish", I ventured.

A concerned look clouded her face.

"We don't open the shop until seven in the mornings." She brightened suddenly. "Still, if you want anything before you go, just ring the bell at the farmhouse and someone will come out and serve you."

She bustled back into the shop and left us looking at each other, slightly stunned that she would be prepared to get out of bed at the crack of dawn to open the shop and sell one of us the Mars Bar he'd forgotten to buy the evening before. If I'd known that, I reflected, and the depth and breadth of the goods contained in May's Aladdin's Cave, I could have saved myself the walk down into Hebden Bridge and all the way back up again. But then I would have missed *Slack Bottom* and that would have been a shame.

The farm's water supply for campers comprised two ancient stone troughs, both set into a stone wall which ran along the northernmost edge of the farmyard. Spring water from the hill flowed below ground and surfaced into the trough on the right, then flowed from that into the slightly lower trough on the left. The right-hand trough, we were informed, was drinking water; the left was set aside for washing. The order was important because if it was reversed the drinking water would become contaminated by the washing of people and clothes. We both consumed quite a bit of that water (from the right-hand trough, obviously) and suffered no ill effects.

The camping field at High Gate Farm was a small, uneven patch of grass with a lane on the farm side of it and a steep slope leading up to the hills on the other. It was bounded by a wire fence, with a small gate to access the lane and the farm. It was also well-sheltered. Mike and I had managed to find two pieces of ground which were level enough for our tents and we spent a warm, comfortable night there, well fed and watered by our visit to the New Delight Inn, a mile or so across the valley.

*****

We set off again next morning, and this was the first time I'd walked any real distance with Mike. I found that he set a testing pace on the flat but that I tended to outpace him on the uphill stretches. I took no pride in that: Mike was ten years older than me, carrying at least twice as much weight in his rucksack and on painkillers for a whiplash injury he'd sustained in a car accident a few months before.

I seem to slip into a natural groove when I'm walking and I would have found it very difficult to slow down in order to accommodate Mike on the uphills. Because of that, I couldn't reasonably expect him to slow down for me on the flats. The cumulative effect of this was Mike dragging me along on the flat and me dragging him up the hills. With me working to keep up with Mike on the flat and him working to keep up with me on the slopes, we moved across the barren moor like an express train. In short, together we made a much better pace than either of us would have done alone.

The sun came out, but never really succeeded in breaking through the low, hazy cloud. It felt continuously as if a scorching-hot day was only a few minutes away, but it always remained just out of reach on the other side of the gloom. Without full sun, the morning was crisp and cold. We threaded our way between more reservoirs and feeder channels, then broke out onto bleak, almost featureless moorland.

We were in Brontë Country, the place where the Brontë sisters lived and set their novels in the early nineteenth century. Today the area is internationally famous as a result, with hordes of tourists flocking to see the sights. The local footpaths across the moors are even signed in Japanese to cater for one of the biggest fan demographics.

Our trail passed Top Withens, now a ruin but once a working farm and believed by many to have featured in *Wuthering Heights.* The plaque on the old farmhouse wall tries to tell the truth while gallantly keeping hope alive for the hardcore devotees:

> TOP WITHENS
> THIS FARMHOUSE HAS BEEN ASSSOCIATED WITH
> "WUTHERING HEIGHTS"
> THE EARNSHAW HOME IN EMILY BRONTË'S
> NOVEL.
> THE BUILDINGS, EVEN WHEN COMPLETE, BORE
> NO RESEMBLANCE TO THE HOUSE SHE
> DESCRIBED.
> BUT THE SITUATION MAY HAVE BEEN IN HER
> MIND WHEN SHE WROTE OF THE MOORLAND
> SETTING OF THE HEIGHTS.

Next was Ponden Hall, dating from 1634 and another inspiration for the Brontës, although for them the views from the lovely old hall must have looked very different without the large Ponden Reservoir next door, built some two and a half centuries after the hall.

I noticed Mike was very disciplined about his walking and it was his habit to stop for a break about every two hours. I liked that: I found it much easier to keep pushing myself to hike when I knew at what time my next break would be. Without that sort of discipline it's all too easy to kid yourself that you need to take break early, or to force yourself to keep walking when a break really is needed.

As we approached Cowling, the subject of our chatter turned to a pub which we both knew was in the village and right on the Pennine Way. The sun was almost out and the closer we got to what we had come to regard as the Cowling Oasis, the more attractive became the idea of sitting outside in the pale sunshine with a fortifying drink and a bag of crisps.

A simple pleasure, you might think, and wish your heroes on, but it was not to be. The Fates had decreed otherwise, almost as if to emphasise to us that fantasy must

The South Pennines

only rarely become reality, and we found the pub had become a kitchen showroom.

I could have lived with a restaurant or a private house, but the change to a kitchen showroom seemed to mock us. "This area is moving up-market," it seemed to say, "And it no longer wishes to associate with people like you."

There was another pub, but it was at the far end of Cowling. Cowling is a linear village, so the far end of it was a respectable distance away. Mike and I were still new to each other, still sizing each other up, but we quickly established that we were like-minded on this issue. A leisurely pint, outside, where we could air our feet, we decided, was not an unreasonable ambition, and we set off through Cowling.

Pausing only to take directions from someone who went out of his way to demonstrate that the tradition of the English village idiot is alive and well, we arrived at The Bay Horse, an old coaching inn which was ideally suited to our simple needs.

A few jars later, refreshed and reinvigorated, it was on to Lothersdale, a small village which has stayed small because it has no mains gas or water, a factor which, not surprisingly, has hindered development and resulted in more than a few law suits about water rights. A quick enquiry in the Hare and Hounds saw us directed to a house named Lynmouth at the far end of the village. "If there's no-one in, nip back and leave the money behind the bar".

Lynmouth was a 1920s-looking villa surrounded by neat, cherished gardens, calm and quiet in the late afternoon sunshine. I knocked on the front door and, when I got no answer, peered through the windows into the dark interior, but no-one was home.

The back lawn was an ideal spot for camping, and Mike and I quickly had our tents up. An outbuilding contained a toilet and a shower. A handwritten note fixed to the wall near the sink informed me that if I wanted hot water in the shower, I'd need to go back outside, run the hosepipe tap for a bit and then turn it off, then go back into the outbuilding and start the shower.

I assessed this advice as unlikely, but the shock of stepping naked into a cold shower after I'd turned the control to *hot* sent me straight back outside to run the hosepipe tap. Mike was sitting outside his tent polishing his boots.

"That was quick," he called out. "Is it a good shower?"

The noise of water spattering onto tarmac made conversation difficult, so I shouted something about "dodgy shower" and "explain later". Bless his heart, Mike didn't seem to worry about what I might be doing naked, firing water all over the driveway from the outside tap when I said I'd gone for a shower. He simply nodded and put the lid back onto his tin of boot polish.

I turned off the hosepipe, legged it back into the shower room and experienced what I can only describe as the shower of the gods, then did some laundry in the sink.

I'd just got my washing pegged out on Lynmouth's washing line and Mike had gone into the now vacant shower room, when a car pulled up and an elderly couple got out. I hoped we'd put our tents in the right place, and that they wouldn't mind that we'd used the shower and the washing line, but they were kindness personified. I paid for both of us, frankly an almost token fee, and Jeanette, the lady I paid, brought us out two coffees on a tray.

The sunshine didn't last, however, and later that evening Mike and I found ourselves running back to Lynmouth from the pub in a desperate attempt to get our dry washing in before the drizzle turned to rain.

We got there to find an empty washing line.

The absence of clean laundry (OK, semi-clean, in my case) was perturbing, the more so because neither of us had much in the way of spare clothing and so couldn't replace it. When you have to carry your possessions all day every day, it's surprising what you discover you can do without. But we needn't have worried: Jeanette had taken it in when the rain started, folded it neatly and placed it in the shower room for us.

It rained hard in the night, but the sound of the rain on my tent didn't bother me. It was a regular, almost reassuring sound and it partially suppressed the noise made by the randy and very loud pheasants, who were enthusiastically copulating in the garden next door.

Breakfast for me the following day was porridge, tea and a Snickers bar. That never seems to be quite enough calories for me on a long walk, but I noticed that Mike was even more economical: his breakfast was a cup of Coke.

The early mist soon lifted and by 6am we found ourselves walking in sunshine under a bright, blue sky. Our way took us uphill to start with, which was no surprise because we'd spent the night in a settlement and in these parts the towns and villages tend to be in the sheltered valley bottoms rather than up on the exposed hill-tops.

The dull moorland quickly gave way to fields and dales. Almost in the blink of an eye, our world had changed from brown to green! We walked uphill through deep-green sheep pastures bounded by dry-stone walls, across fields and then joined the Leeds and Liverpool Canal just before East Marton.

This section of the canal dates from 1793, although the whole thing didn't open until 1816. The canal passes under a curious double-arched bridge at East Marton, where one of the arches is directly on top of the other. It looks very much as if a giant had picked up a stone bridge and carefully placed it on top of an existing stone bridge. The second, uppermost arch was built on top of the old bridge to facilitate motor traffic when the old pack-horse track was transformed into an A road for cars and lorries.

I enjoy canal-side walking, but unfortunately for me the Leeds and Liverpool was soon behind us and we slipped into Gargrave for a quick re-supply at the Co-op. The ball of my left foot had started troubling me so I dealt with it early and taped it up. I hoped it wouldn't stop me from keeping up with Mike on the level parts of the path because I was pleased with the progress we were making and I found myself enjoying his company.

As we crossed the fields on the way out of Gargrave, I watched Mike checking our route. I'd noticed that his method of navigation was different to mine and that interested me, so I studied him to assess and, maybe, to copy his system.

My preferred method is always to know exactly where I am on my map, and what features I have coming up ahead of me. Whenever there's any doubt or if the weather starts to close in, out comes my compass and I check my heading frequently. I pack so that my map and compass are readily available at all times when I'm walking, so that it's never a chore to get to them and use them.

Mike, I noticed, walked for long periods with a guidebook in his hand. He consulted it often and when it wasn't in his hand, it was tucked into a trouser pocket on his right thigh. He only used one walking pole, so as to leave one hand free for the guidebook. That approach gave him a lot of detailed information to navigate with. He got the bigger picture by occasional use of his compass; but he didn't use the compass in the precise "bearing to the nearest degree" manner that I did. He would look at his guide book then turn to me and say something like, "We need to follow that valley, the one that runs north-west," and then start walking.

I like watching people who are good at something and I'll happily crib their ideas if they look good. I took on board Mike's method of casual but frequent use of the compass and it has served me well. I still get my detail from the map and I still use my compass for precise bearings, but now, only when I need to. *Borrow with pride!* That's my motto.

Chapter 6

The Yorkshire Dales

We get muddled in Malham. – Taking a punt on Pen-y-ghent. – The ultimate man-cave. – Disaster in the dale. – Contrasts in customer service.

John Hillaby was of the opinion that the most spectacular part of the Pennine Way starts at Gargrave. That might be an overly-harsh judgement on some of the other sections, and of course it's completely subjective: so much depends on the weather, the state of the walker's feet and a hundred and one other variables, but it is fair to say that the landscape after Gargrave is pretty spectacular.

Mike and I reached the River Aire and began following it. As we did so, the route changed again as we passed rural watermills and walked across neat little mill leets. This was an idyllic, rustic setting and it was a shock to the system when our path suddenly tipped us out into a huge car park in a field on the edge of Malham.

We paused, somewhat bewildered, trying to work out our route through the rows and rows of cars, shiny in the sunshine but incongruous in the large green field. There were picnickers and day-trippers everywhere; elderly couples, families chasing staggering toddlers, sullen teenagers standing about studying their mobile phones. Welcome back to the twenty-first century! I looked at Mike.

"What the hell's going on here? Some sort of festival or something?"

He shrugged. "Tourists, I expect."

"Tourists? Touring what? What is there round here for tourists?"

Mike was more knowledgeable than me. "Malham Cove, probably."

Of course. The great limestone cliff to the north of Malham, and the source of the River Aire. John Hillaby called it, "The gateway to the great Pennine moors." I'd never seen Malham Cove, but even so I was surprised it drew so many people. I've been to the Grand Canyon and it was less crowded than Malham.

We found the main street and plonked ourselves down at a table outside the Buck Inn with our customary shandies. Malham was our intended destination for the day and it had a couple of campsites for us to choose from. Day-walkers and tourists teemed and swarmed around us as we drank thirstily outside the pub. Mike checked his guidebook and I looked at my map.

We decided to camp on a farm on the other side of town. It was a lovely campsite, well-maintained with clean, spacious showers and toilets. I like to pay on arrival, so that I can then forget about money, so I followed a series of home-made laminated signs which directed would-be campers around the farmhouse and to the door of a conservatory which was built onto the back of it. Inside, the farmer had taken up what was obviously his customary station during the period when most campers check in. A large man in a collarless shirt, he was sprawled in a chair in the hot conservatory, working his way through a six-pack of beer and handing a paper camping permit to anyone who gave him seven pounds.

I felt tired as I lay in my tent and thought back over the day. I could have done with more canal walking, I decided. Or a conservatory and a six-pack. I drifted off to sleep wondering if the good weather could hold. I was walking through the rainiest part of England. I couldn't get away with more dry days - could I?

*****

I made another early start with Mike the next morning and we reached the top of Malham Cove as the sun was coming up. It had the makings of a lovely day.

Malham Cove is an 80m limestone cliff and it was formed by meltwater from glaciers at the end of the last ice age 12,000 years BCE. Now, the ice has gone and the water runs underneath the permeable limestone, but in the ice age the limestone became saturated and then it froze. In a state of permafrost it behaved like impermeable rock, and water flowed across it rather than soaking into it, resulting in the feature which so many people visit today. It must have been a massive waterfall.

We picked our way carefully across the limestone pavement at the top of the Cove, a GCSE geography textbook example, clints, grikes and all, and started up the valley behind it, still in deep shadow that early in the morning.

For me, the Dales proved the most beautiful part of the walk thus far. Green fields and dry-stone walls feel more welcoming to me than swampy moorland ground with miles of peat bog. The Dales created a richer, less bleak impression on the mind.

To the left was Fountains Fell, so called because in the 1200s it was owned by the Cistercian monks of Fountains Abbey, 40km to the east. The monks used it for grazing sheep, but coal was mined extensively here from 1790 to 1860, and used for lead smelting. The area is littered with old mine shafts, some still open and others filled in haphazardly in a half-arsed sort of way. Signs warn hikers of the dangers and implore you to keep to the path.

I walked up ancient trackways between old stone walls, with Mike falling back behind me, only to catch me up again when the path levelled out. We skirted deep limestone gorges and wrapped ourselves up against the cold wind.

After a time, the sun broke through. Blue skies, high clouds and strong winds accompanied us as we wound our way down the valley on the approach to Pen-y-ghent, looming large on the other side in front of us.

I found myself starting to resent Pen-y-ghent. To start with, I could see that it was a steep climb to the summit at 694m. Now that's just about acceptable when there's a need for it, but our destination for the day was Horton-in-Ribblesdale. Horton was pretty much straight ahead, but instead of going directly to Horton, the Pennine Way goes around three sides of a square to reach it, a route which includes the ascent and descent of Pen-y-ghent. Deviating so far from the obvious natural route felt somewhat forced, an impression cemented by the fact that if we wanted to walk the Pennine Way, we had no option but to follow it around those three sides of a square and then, and only then, down into Horton. It all felt … unnecessary, my brain moaned to me. That was it: unnecessary. A bit too much "because it's there". Starting to get tired at this stage, I honestly don't know what I would have done had Mike suggested a shortcut.

Despite my unspoken complaints, Pen-y-ghent was on the Pennine Way and it had to be climbed, so I said a rude word and started up the track ahead of me, Mike falling behind very quickly on this steep climb. The wind was even stronger as I got higher and, on the third quarter of the climb, I had to stop and stow my trekking poles so that I could use my hands.

I topped out and took in the views while I waited for Mike. I felt sorry for anyone who had cut out this section of the Pennine Way and hiked straight on to Horton: I was looking at stunning views across a vast, empty landscape. What was it

The Yorkshire Dales

I said about mankind being fickle?

I had to wait a long time for Mike to join me. Like me, he'd had to scramble the last part of the climb. The wind was so strong, he told me, that part way up it blew his glasses clean off his face. He'd only saved them by a reflex catch. We found a seat in the stone shelter and dug out something to eat.

We dropped down from Pen-y-ghent on the path to Horton, gently at first, across the dry, rough grassland, then more steeply down a gravel track, the strong wind behind us pushing us forward.

When Alfred Wainwright passed through Horton-in-Ribblesdale in 1938[2], his guidebook informed him that there were three pubs. Try as he might, he could only find two of them. Rural pubs might be struggling and Horton is only a small village, but it still provides enough custom to sustain the same two pubs (unlike AW, two pubs were enough for me, so I didn't even look for the third). Mike and I got some drinks at the Crown and took our glasses outside to a spot where we could sit in the sunshine but out of the wind.

With morale duly bolstered, we set off through the village to the campsite at Holme Farm.

There were already a few small tents in the camping field when we arrived. Mike wandered into the field for a look around and I found the owner, Chris, in Reception.

"Reception" was a large tunnel-tent the size of a small house. It was anchored to the ground by thick ropes attached to waist-high stakes and it was nothing like any tent I'd ever seen. To start with, you couldn't miss Reception: immediately outside of it a row of flags fluttered from full-size flag poles, making it look more like the Council of Europe than a campsite. It was big and semi-permanent, which was just as well because it looked as if Chris, a very affable man in his

---

[2] *A walking trip beautifully described in the book* A Pennine Journey.

eighties, lived there. The place was crammed with old furniture, much of it antique in appearance, some gilt, some deep-polished wood. On the practical side there was a fridge, a freezer, a microwave oven and a gas ring. Decorative china and glassware sparkled from the side units and a large England flag above the piano carried the legend, "Chris's Champagne Chateau." You couldn't miss the piano because it stood next to the organ and the oil paintings, while overhead a sumptuous damask-style fabric formed a ceiling like that in a Bedouin tent, snapping and billowing in the wind. As if that wasn't enough, it was the only "tent" I've ever seen that had proper, sealed-unit uPVC double-glazing.

It was quite simply the biggest and the best man-cave in the entire world. I'd only gone in there for a minute, to pay for a night's camping, but I stepped back outside with my senses buzzing, feeling as if I'd spent a full day in an eclectic, mad combination of the National Gallery and Disneyland. For some reason I couldn't describe, it was uplifting.

Back on the camping field I chose a site as sheltered from the wind as I could and pitched my tent. Mike already had his tent up on the next pitch and after an exchange of pleasantries, he made his way over to the man-cave to pay his camping fee.

After I'd put my tent up, taking particular care to drive the pegs in firmly and keep the guys taut because of the wind, I carefully organised my kit inside it. My tent was "one-person" in size and weighed just 560g, a great attribute if you have to carry it for ten or twelve hours a day. It was spacious and had proved strong in wind and rain, so I had confidence in it. It set up with one of my trekking poles as the single tent pole, with a twelve inch carbon fibre tube slotted onto the tip of the trekking pole to give the pole the height required to support the tent. I'd got quite practised at pitching it, so it was the work of a moment to set up my home for the night. I grabbed my towel and soap and headed for the toilet block.

The Yorkshire Dales

When I got back, Mike was back at his tent. The wind was now raging across the camping field in short but brutal gusts. Mike waved me over to him. I leaned into the wind and walked across the grass. We both squatted down in the lea of Mike's tent.

"Did you meet Chris, the owner?"

"Yes," I told him. "Lovely bloke. That's one hell of an office he's got, isn't it?"

Mike had a vaguely startled look about him and spoke to me in a low voice, as if imparting a confidence.

"I went in there to pay for the camping and he gave me a big glass of whisky. Then he asked if I was hungry and cooked me eggs and bacon. I told him I had food but he just got on with it and stuck it in front of me. It was lovely."

"I thought he seemed like a nice bloke," I offered.

But Mike wasn't finished.

"He'd only charged a few quid, so I thought I'd better pay him for the food but he wouldn't hear of it. It must have cost him more than I'd paid to camp, so I tried again. I said I'd pay and asked him what it cost. Do you know what he said?"

"What did he say?"

"'Same as the sunshine lad, same as the sunshine.'"

I smiled.

My tent was behind me as I chatted with Mike, and he nodded towards it.

"Look what the wind's doing to your tent. You'd better get over there."

I turned around and what I saw made me stop smiling. A gust of wind was roaring over the field and my tent seemed to be the only thing stopping it from passing on down the dale and out into the rest of Yorkshire. The tent fabric ballooned with the wind, holding it like the sails do on a racing yacht, distorting the whole structure and making it a grotesque parody of what a tent should look like. I wasn't unduly worried, because I knew the tent fabric and guy-lines were very strong and unlikely to break, and I'd taken care to put the pegs in properly. It might look disturbing, but what could go wrong?

No more than a second elapsed before I found out exactly what could go wrong. My trekking pole deformed under the intense pressure from the tent-cum-sail and there was an audible "crack" as the carbon fibre pole-extender on top of it splintered. The tent went down like an elephant shot by poachers and lay there, fluttering pathetically on the ground as though waiting for someone to put it out of its misery. I ran to it and started to pick through the remains.

After a little thinking, I made some adjustments and managed to re-set the tent without the pole extender, although this meant that my "tent pole" was now twelve inches shorter than it needed to be. As a consequence the tent had to be pitched lower, markedly reducing the room available to me inside it.

I was annoyed. I still had many miles to go and many nights to sleep in this tent and I wanted it the way it was when I put it up, not like this, a bodged job with a cramped interior.

Earlier that evening a chap named Dave, from the other side of the campsite, had come over to take a look at my tent. He was planning to buy one like it, he said, to walk the 1,900 mile Te Araroa Trail in New Zealand. Once I'd reset it, Dave noticed the change in my tent and stopped by again, and we mulled over what had happened.

Once I had completed my emergency adjustments and satisfied myself that I still had a home, albeit not as much of one as I would have preferred, I made myself a cup of tea and had a think.

I'd ordered my tent from a company in Florida. They are known amongst American hikers for the high quality of their customer service, so maybe it was time to find out if this would also apply to the UK? I dug out my phone and called my girlfriend, Debbie. I explained what had happened and asked her to contact the makers of the tent for help. Then, in line with the finest traditions of British hiking, I went to the pub.

Two hours later I was fed and watered, and back on the campsite, tweaking my tent to make sure it would stay the course. Given the time difference between the UK and the US, I didn't expect Debbie to have made much progress but I fancied a chat, so I rang her.

It turned out that plenty had been happening while I was sitting on my backside in the pub. Debbie had checked the maker's website and found that they didn't take telephone calls, only emails, so she'd emailed them. She described what had happened and marked her email "urgent". Within an hour she had received a reply apologising profusely and telling her that a complete new pole (not just a short trekking pole extender) was in the post, sent by express delivery with no charge for the pole or for the delivery. It should be with her, they said, within 48 hours. Now that's what I call customer service. Before I did anything else, I felt obliged to walk across the field and update Dave so that he knew he could rely on these people while he was in New Zealand.[3] Then I wandered back to socialise with Mike for a while before bed.

Mike was disappointed to find that there was no village shop in Horton. At one time, he told me, there had been fourteen shops in this small village. Now there are none. A sign of the times, I guess, but I didn't have time to dwell on it because a new problem was developing.

While we'd been at the pub, a large group of teenagers from two minibuses had joined us on the campsite. The youths soon took over the whole site, playing football between the tents, slamming the minibus doors, and shouting and arguing with each other. Rather than being on an organised trip, it was

---

[3] *The new pole did indeed get from Florida to the UK within 48 hours. Unfortunately, Parcelforce then took a week to move it from one side of London to the other.*

as if they had been turned loose. The fact that many other people were also camping here and, by this time of the evening, were trying to sleep, either escaped their notice or, if they did realise, they simply didn't care. They had a few adults with them but the adults did nothing to moderate their behaviour or exercise any control.

I lay in my tent trying to keep my temper while, outside, a girl called Tracey loudly told an overenthusiastic suitor to "fuck off" and then climbed into one of the vans and slammed the door.

A football bounced off my tent for the umpteenth time and the shouts of the football players stopped during the resulting pause in play as someone ran over to get the ball. Tracey slid back the minibus door with a bang and started a loud phone conversation with a friend, most of it centring on the shortcomings of her admirer.

I told myself that I was young once.

But by the time this nonsense had been going on for over an hour while I was trying to sleep, any empathy I felt had dissipated. When a football hit my tent yet again and rolled down it to rest by the door, I grabbed the door open. One of the football enthusiasts jogged over to get it. He scooped up the ball right in front of me as if I wasn't there and turned to re-join the game.

That was it.

"Oi!" I shouted. The ball carrier paused and turned to make eye contact with me, a surprised look on his face. I wondered if he'd ever had his behaviour challenged before. I pointed at him to reinforce my message and spoke loudly and clearly, so that as many people as possible could hear what I had to say. Just a couple of sentences was all it took. Short and pithy. Even Tracey heard it, over by the minibus.

There were an awful lot more of them than there was of me and I was quite prepared for an adverse reaction, for the remainder of my stay to be made difficult as a result, but I

The Yorkshire Dales

wasn't prepared to take it anymore. After my intervention, though, it was as if they suddenly realised that other people were present after all: the noise reduced to a gentle background hum and not one football hit my tent. Even so, I went to sleep with a feeling of annoyance. Why did it fall to me to sort out other people's behaviour?

Whatever my thoughts on the matter, it obviously did fall to me because next morning three people, unconnected to each other, came to my tent and thanked me.

Keen to be on our way, Mike and I set off bright and early. The weather failed to follow our example. High, solid cloud and no direct sunlight made for a cold start and I kept my jacket on. The scenery, however, did not disappoint, as we tracked up slowly but surely, along old packhorse trails.

The ball of my left foot was still uncomfortable, despite my best efforts at foot-care. I'd kept my feet clean, well-aired and dry, and I'd diligently taped and protected the sore spot. In fact, I'd done everything that should encourage it to improve and I felt a little bit cheated that it didn't seem to be getting any better. That said, it didn't seem to be getting any worse either. Every day in which it didn't get worse just served to convince me that it must get better soon.

My spirits lifted when I saw a red squirrel on a bare patch of limestone near the path. I signalled to Mike to be quiet and then pointed at it, and we stood and watched it, trying not to move or make a noise. After it had entertained us for a few minutes, it scooted out of the streambed in which it had been foraging and disappeared amongst the bracken, the colour of which exactly matched its fur. The effect of this was to hide it in an instant.

We reached Cam End and turned onto Cam High Road, the old Roman road that runs almost all the way to Hawes.

Off to the left I could see the splendour of the Ribblehead Viaduct on the Settle to Carlisle railway, its twenty-four arches standing proud across the dale. The viaduct is 400m long and

32m high. Started in 1870, it took a thousand navvies four years to build it and about a hundred of them died during the process, a shocking death rate by modern standards.

I stood and looked at the graceful structure, away in the distance. It is undoubtedly a beautiful piece of engineering, but was it ever worth a hundred lives? I'd say not, but I live in the twenty-first century, when no civil engineering project would be deemed worthwhile if it carried such an awful human cost. Attitudes were different in the 1870s though. The navvies and their families lived in shanty towns out on the moor; and along with the hundred men who died building the viaduct, another hundred family members are buried in the local churchyard.

It was mid-afternoon on market day when we reached Hawes. We picked our way between stalls and shoppers, and secured a table outside a pub for what was becoming our customary end-of-day pint. It had become a warm day, although still overcast, and we sat outdoors comfortably, watching the busy little town bustling around us.

Our campsite was a farm about a mile out of town, and we were their only customers. With my tent jury-rigged, because of the broken pole-extender, I sat in it, took off my shoes and inspected my feet. In the middle of the ball of my left foot I found that I had a blister on top of a blister and I realised that my foot was deteriorating.

The irritating thing was that I couldn't work out why this was happening. And without working out why it was happening, I couldn't determine the most effective way to deal with it. My shoes had never blistered me before; and each foot had the same type of sock on it, the same type of insole underneath it, and was in the same model of shoe. So why had one foot blistered when the other hadn't?

I was wondering what to do about this when Mike appeared. He was going for water and he wanted to know if I needed any. I showed him my foot. He looked at it for a second and then looked at the insoles I'd pulled out of my shoes when

The Yorkshire Dales

I cleaned them. What he said next solved my problem.

"It looks to me as if that blister is in exactly the same place as the centre of the circular pattern on your insole."

"What? What pattern?"

I grabbed the offending insole. He was right. When the insole was inside the shoe, directly under my blister was a small, circular protrusion which formed the centre of a concentric circular pattern on the base of the insole. It was too much of a coincidence and the scales fell from my eyes.

"I reckon you're right," I told him.

I thought for a second.

"We passed a chemist in town. I'll see if I can pick up some new ones."

As well as a chemist's shop, we'd seen some nice tearooms in Hawes, so instead of making tea at the campsite we walked back into town for a cup. I made sure to call in at the chemist's on the way.

The chemist was a helpful man in his thirties, neatly dressed, wearing a tie and a waistcoat. I explained my problem and showed him the old insole. He ummed and aahed over it for a few seconds and then produced a selection of insoles for my perusal. They were modestly priced but they didn't look much better than those I already had until, with a flourish, he produced the stars of the show, a pair of American-made insoles with plenty of gel cushioning and no pattern to mess up my feet. I immediately thought of something Oliver Hardy used to say to Stan Laurel: "Now we're getting someplace!"

I asked how much they were, and my salesman inclined his head and mumbled inaudibly into his tie, as if a little embarrassed. That caused me to think they were probably very expensive, so I picked them up to check the price tag. My foot hurt and I had a credit card in my pocket - I was determined to solve this problem come what may.

The insoles were the most expensive in the shop, at £14.98. A trifling sum compared to the relief they offered. I paid cash and the helpful chemist seemed almost embarrassed to take my money, although I would have happily paid double to rid myself the discomfort I'd been walking with. After tea, I cut my new insoles to size with my penknife and fitted them into my shoes. Later that evening, when Mike and I walked back into town for a pub dinner, I felt like I was walking on air. And that was before we'd got to the pub.

A good meal, a quiet, comfortable place to pitch the tent and the resolution of my foot problem all combined to give me a good night's sleep.

Mike must have felt the same, because we were on the move by 6am.

We walked north out of Hawes while the town was still fast asleep, then turned north-west across short, green grass, through stone-walled sheep pastures. We were walking in Wensleydale, home of the eponymous cheese, which explained the Wensleydale cheese factory we'd walked past in Hawes the day before. As we walked, we startled lambs and rabbits, and they fled before us. The sky was bright but grey, with a haze in the far distance.

As we got higher, the amount of green grass around us decreased and the coverage of brown hill-grass increased. We were climbing Great Shunner Fell, nearly 500m higher than Hawes.

Great Shunner Fell has many false summits, each of which can easily delude a walker into believing that he's nearly at the top, only to disappoint as the next "summit" hoves into view. As if that wasn't challenging enough, the wind got stronger and stronger as we got higher, until it was difficult to stand upright.

We reached the top and paused to look around. Coal was mined extensively up here for many years and you can still see the occasional piece of it on the summit.

Some very shrewd person has built a stone windbreak in the shape of a plus sign on the summit, with bench seats built-in. The design means that it's always possible to get out of the wind no matter which direction it blows from. Feeling grateful, I took a seat out of the wind and pulled my water bottle out of my rucksack pocket.

I knew there was another aircraft crash site on the east side of Great Shunner Fell, but I couldn't see any trace of it. In January 1943 a Canadian Halifax crashed here. One of the crew, Sergeant Pudney, rescued his colleagues from the plane and walked two miles to Thwaite to get help. Pudney was awarded the George Medal but sadly never received it: he was killed six months later, flying in another Halifax when it crashed after being struck by lightning near Kings Lynn.

I'd been on top of Great Shunner Fell for five minutes when I realised that Mike might not see me as he crested the hill. I was on the opposite side of the cruciform windbreak and if Mike stayed on the path and didn't look over the top, he could walk right on by without noticing me.

I jumped up and looked back the way I'd come. No sign of Mike. That was odd; he wasn't that far behind. I turned to my left just in time to see Mike's back disappearing past me. He had walked past without looking over the top of the windbreak. I shouted, he turned, and we both took a break out of the wind.

I was stuffing a chocolate bar into my face as fast as I could swallow it, when Mike turned to me.

"You're a much faster walker than me and I feel like I'm holding you back. I don't mind if you want to go on ahead."

That caught me by surprise. I thought for a second. Was Mike fed up with walking with me? Was he saying that he'd prefer me to walk on so that he could continue solo? Or was I reading too much into it? I thought honesty was the best policy.

"I don't feel like you're holding me back."

Mike continued, "You've dragged me up these hills and I'm grateful, but I'm slower and I don't want to hold you back."

"I'm thinking quite the opposite. I might be quicker *up*

the hills, but that's my natural pace and it would be hard to slow it down. But you consistently aim to walk further than I would each day, so if anything, you've dragged me further along the Pennine Way each day. Maybe it's swings and roundabouts?"

That seemed to placate him and we got up to start the downhill into Thwaite.

My data sheet told me there was a café in Thwaite, and the village was too small to make finding it difficult. As we arrived there the sun was just breaking through the cloud and we settled ourselves at a table outside. Mike went to check the door and I heard him rattle the handle.

"Oh no! It's closed!"

I pointed to a sign near the door.

"There's a sign there. What time does it say they open?"

Mike put his glasses on and bent forward to read the sign.

"Eleven o'clock. What time is it now?"

I checked my watch.

"Ten fifty-eight."

He smiled.

"That's timing, that is."

We'd crossed into the next dale, and we were now in upper Swaledale. The area was starting to look familiar to me from my Coast to Coast walk two years earlier, because the Pennine Way crosses the Coast to Coast Walk at Keld, about 5km from where we were sitting.

After a brace of cooked breakfasts we straightened out limbs which had stiffened while we sat, and started off again. To get to Keld we had to climb Kisdon, a steep-sided hill a couple of hundred metres higher than Thwaite. Our path went diagonally up the hillside and then turned north towards Keld. We walked surrounded by banks of primroses, Swaledale dropping away to our right, the sides of the dale bare, the floor a patchwork pattern delineated by stone walls and barns.

The waterfalls at Keld provided a pleasant spot to fuel up, then we set off up West Stones Dale, heading for the highest

The Yorkshire Dales

pub in England, the Tan Hill Inn. Our path followed the contours along the east side of the dale, but from the frequent mentions of tarmac in his book, I think Wainwright must have used the road to the west of us when he walked here. Wainwright recalled walking through thick fog until he reached the pub sign, then casting about for the pub itself. Eventually he found it on the other side of the road, unnoticed until that point, so thick was the fog.

We could see the Tan Hill Inn as we rounded Lad Gill Head, just over a mile away from it. Mike and I had walked together along the contour path in West Stones Dale but, as was our wont, I'd drifted ahead as we climbed to Stonesdale Moor and Mike had dropped back.

In front of me, about halfway to the inn, I could see a group of walkers, apparently heading for a large coach which was parked outside. I was about to wait for Mike but then some vague, undefined impulse seized me and I set off towards the group of ramblers, intent on reaching the pub before they did. I tried to justify it in my mind by telling myself that it made sense to get there before the crowd, so that I could get the beers in without the necessity to queue behind twenty people, but I knew in my heart that it was pure competition: they had a head start, but even after a long day's walking I would still get to the pub before they did.

The path turned into a track and I came down it like an express train, secretly pleased that I still had this in me after 200km of hill and dale.

I passed the day-walkers at pace, throwing out a few cheery greetings as I passed them and receiving the same back in return. I reached the pub several lengths ahead of the competition and went straight into the public bar. I paid for two people to camp overnight, had the beers on a table and was halfway through mine and thinking about another one by the time the day-walkers arrived. Fortunately for me, and for Mike when he eventually reached the pub, the walkers I'd passed had pre-booked *en masse* and they all trooped into a separate function room for their dinner, leaving the public bar free for us.

Chapter 7

The North Pennines

Toughing it out at Tan Hill. – Mike's philosophy of life. – Cold showers, cod and chips. – Cow Green: lost to the nation? – The grandeur of High Cup. – The gift of Greg's Hut. – Kindness at the railway café.

When I crossed the road outside the pub in order to enter it, I'd stepped out of the Yorkshire Dales National Park and into the North Pennines Area of Outstanding Natural Beauty.

At that point on the map there was no perceptible difference between the two. I'd walked across the Yorkshire Dales National Park once before and had been hugely impressed with it, but the North Pennines were new to me. After the Battle of Waterloo, the Duke of Wellington said that he'd spent most of his career wondering what was on the other side of the hill. As I sipped my beer and waited for Mike, I too wondered what was on the other side of the hill and what the future held. Unlike the Iron Duke, I couldn't set up a cadre of "exploring officers" to reconnoitre it for me – I'd have to walk it myself.

One of the bar staff put some wood on the fire and the flames leapt up quickly, and started crackling loudly.

My surroundings were clearly old and had obviously been a travellers' refuge for centuries. The Tan Hill Inn dates back to the 1600s and in the 1700s it was used by miners digging coal in the area. Until the 1930s it was surrounded by cottages, but these were demolished just before Wainwright called here in 1938, their demolition creating the splendid isolation in which the building now stands.

My reverie was interrupted by the door opening, and Mike peered in. We took it easy in the bar for a while and then went out to look at the camping field. It wasn't the best we'd encountered on the Pennine Way to date.

Maybe my expectations were high because the Tan Hill Inn is such an iconic location, or maybe I caught it at a bad time, but the inn's camping site wasn't quite what I was expecting.

It was uneven, which is never a good attribute if you have to lie down on it to go to sleep, and open to the wind, which was whistling across it unchecked from the east. The area was strewn with wind-blown litter interspersed with occasional bottles and glasses, presumably from the bar. The scene was made even more gloomy by the desolate moorland surrounding it, the fading light and what looked like a distant mist creeping slowly but inexorably up the valley towards us. If what I was looking at had been a wild-camping option I would have walked on and looked for somewhere flatter and more sheltered, but the prospect of a decent cooked meal, a warm fire and a flush toilet was a powerful draw and so I followed Mike onto the grass, looking for the least unsuitable place to put up my tent.

I wondered why they didn't put up anything to block the wind, but why would they? Any development could only come with a cost, but the slight improvement resulting would hardly justify putting up the camping fees to recoup that cost. And anything built or put up would have to be maintained, which would also come at a cost. A few hours' litter picking would have improved the place immeasurably but, again, litter collection is work which would result in no increase in income and so not worth doing. It looked as if the subject of economics was going to be responsible for a pretty average night's camping.

I chose the flattest and least exposed part of the field I could find, removed a handful of shards of broken glass, hoping that I hadn't left any behind to pierce my groundsheet, and put up my tent. Mike did the same. I cleaned myself up and checked my blister, then went to the grimy campers' toilet and rinsed out a pair of socks. I didn't know if I'd get them dry in time to wear them, but I prefer even wet socks to socks with dirt and grit in them. Suitably organised and with our admin tasks completed, we went back into the warm pub for dinner, in my case with the nagging worry that the persistent wind might blow my tent down as it had done in Horton a few days ago.

The pub was cosy and we spent a pleasant evening with a couple out for dinner on their wedding anniversary. If they saw anything odd about including a pair of grubby hikers on their special evening, they were too polite to show it. Hospitable as they were, we excused ourselves from them after a decent interval, more so that we could be satisfied we weren't intruding than due to any disinclination to their company.

When we were quietly seated at our own table, Mike aired something that had been lingering on his mind.

"You're a much faster walker than me. I was watching you today - it's that long stride. Going uphill, I take two paces to every one of yours. I know I'm holding you back."

I thought we'd dealt with this topic, so I was surprised that it had surfaced once more.

"I don't feel like you're holding me back. I know I shot downhill to the pub yesterday, but something got into me and I couldn't slow down."

Mike smiled. He was a long-distance walker and he knew.

"That will have been the coach party. No, it's not that.

Not many people walk faster than me, but you do. You should go on alone. You'd finish this walk much quicker without me."

I'd been doing some thinking too, so I set the thing out from my perspective.

I know that many hikers like to walk alone. The phrase "hike your own hike" has become so well-known that it's virtually a doctrine for living as well as a trekking epithet. I understood completely that Mike might want to walk on his own. As a walker, I have to say there's no offence taken or intended by that: when a path has to be walked, sometimes a person must walk it solo. That's not a negative reflection on their friends and acquaintances, it's simply a fact.

I also know that I set a reasonable pace when I'm walking. Mike was slower, but I didn't feel that he was holding me back; quite the opposite, in fact.

I'd planned twenty-one days to walk the 423km of the Pennine Way including travelling and a couple of rest days, the latter being completely free of walking to keep me mentally and physically fresh. I knew, because Mike had told me, that he had just sixteen days to complete the walk. As a result of this time constraint, Mike had two options. He could walk hard and make sure that he completed the Pennine Way in the sixteen days he had allotted, or he could walk for sixteen days and finish wherever he found himself.

Every morning, when we'd discussed the place we hoped to reach by the end of that day, Mike's intended walk had proved to be longer than mine. I'd stuck with him and walked more than I'd planned each day as a result. I might be dragging Mike up the steep sections, but he was dragging me along the whole Pennine Way.

I knew that if I stayed with Mike I would have to sacrifice my rest days, so I'd had to decide the most beneficial option for me. I could take my rest days and profit from them, but I would lose Mike in the process. Alternatively, I could keep walking with Mike and enjoy his companionship, in which case I'd have to forgo the rest days and the recuperative opportunities they offered. My objective was to complete the Pennine Way and to enjoy it, so I'd been mentally weighing up those two options to work out which of them would best assist me towards my goal.

An impartial reader might aver that my approach was somewhat selfish and I don't think I could wriggle completely free from such a charge. In mitigation, I'd ask you to consider the reason I was there. I wasn't about to camp in a storm, outside the highest pub in England, in a tent with a broken tent pole purely for the fun of it. Neither was I there to walk *part* of the Pennine Way. My goal was to walk the whole thing, all 423km from Edale to Kirk Yetholm. In addition, I knew it wouldn't all be beer and skittles, but I intended to get as much enjoyment from the experience as I could.

After much deliberation I had decided that walking with Mike would contribute more to my chances of finishing the Pennine Way than walking alone would and, at the same time, the pleasure of his company would add to my enjoyment.

Mike looked relieved when I said this and I realised that he hadn't been trying to ditch me. The idea that he was getting me further along the trail than I would otherwise be seemed to allay his worry that he was holding me back. He went on to tell me that this confirmed what he had been thinking for a few days.

I asked what he'd been thinking for a few days.

"This is going to sound weird and I hope it doesn't offend you."

I'm a pretty easy-going sort of bloke and I couldn't think of anything the mild-mannered Mike could say which would be likely to upset me. Add the fact that I'd just had a good dinner and a couple of pints, with the expectation of a cosy down sleeping bag before me, and, frankly, the prospect of Mike pushing me to the point where I kicked off in a crowded bar seemed unlikely.

I told Mike that there were no guarantees, but that I'd try to keep a grip on myself.

Suitably reassured, Mike went on to tell me that he believed I had been sent to help him complete the Pennine Way. In his experience of life, and I'm summarising greatly here, whenever he came up against difficulty or danger, some sort of assistance, he knew not from where, was provided to help him overcome his obstacles. Mike wasn't sure that he believed in a god or angels, but there was definitely, he felt, a benevolent force watching over him and helping him through times of adversity. When the going got tough, someone or something would be sent, he wasn't sure by whom, to help him through. On this occasion, he felt, I was that divine agent.

My initial reaction was amazement that anyone could seriously believe such gibberish in this day and age. In the Middle Ages maybe, but in the twenty-first century? Surely not.

Despite my surprise at Mike's disclosure, I kept it to myself. He'd made a very personal admission to me and I didn't want to upset him. I find other people's beliefs interesting, though, so I ventured a few questions.

"Right. OK. Please don't take this as a criticism, but exactly what evidence do you have for this belief?"

Mike went on to expound his thoughts at some length. For him, it all centred on his feelings and his convictions, and he was cheerful about the complete lack of anything external and concrete which might back up his ideas. He felt watched over and protected and those feelings convinced him that he *was* watched over and protected. At various times he had experienced feelings which persuaded him of the existence of ghosts and spirits, and he found their presence sustaining and comforting.

I'd started out trying be non-judgemental as I listened to Mike, but I found it increasingly difficult to maintain that approach as he went on. The intensity and complexity of his philosophy of life combined with the absence of anything to support it made me wonder if he was a little unhinged. I thought about my reaction and realised that I found the sincerity of his beliefs unsettling not because of what he believed, but because he asserted that it was so but provided no objective evidence and plainly did not desire any. I found myself making a conscious mental effort to remember the bloke who had slogged across the hills with me, the chap I'd sat outside pubs with and who had put his tent up next to mine. Mike was all right. A bit wacky in places, maybe, but all right.

Some "spiritual" folk are fond of saying that absence of evidence is not evidence of absence: the fact that there's no evidence of ghosts and gods doesn't mean they don't exist. I mulled over what Mike was telling me but I wasn't drawn to it. Thinking about philosophies for life, I prefer Bertram Russell's teapot test. Russell held that if someone asserts something is true, it is up to them to prove it, not up to others to disprove it. He used the analogy of a teapot orbiting the sun, too small to be detected by humans. There's no evidence of its existence but, at the same time, its existence cannot be disproved. Common sense, however, tells us it isn't there and the burden of proof rests with anyone who insists it is.

I hadn't expected any divine revelation when Mike started talking, but I was disappointed that it was all, "Because I think…," "Because I feel…," and so on. I tried a different tack to try to better understand what he was telling me.

"Mike, the average life expectancy in the UK for men is 79. I might live even longer. Are you saying all of that is purely so I could be sent here to help you finish the Pennine Way in sixteen days?"

That wasn't what he was saying. He wasn't suggesting that my sole purpose in life was to help him cover the 423km between Edale and Kirk Yetholm. However, he did believe that, knowing he was struggling to complete the Pennine Way in the time he'd allocated, some sort of divine intervention had been arranged to help him.

As is often the case with any discussion about personal or religious beliefs, I thought, there seemed no logic to this.

"If I've been sent to help you because you only allowed yourself sixteen days, who or what would they have sent if you'd only allowed yourself two days to walk the whole thing?"

"Then I'd fail because of my own stupidity."

"So sixteen days is deserving of help, but two would be stupidity? Where does god draw the line? Eight days, for instance – would eight days be deserving of help or would eight days be stupid?"

Mike corrected me. He wasn't sure he believed in a god and he didn't know where the line would be drawn, but he knew that help came to him when he needed it and he believed the help that he got was spiritual in origin. He needed help on the Pennine Way and I had been sent.

An element of solipsism was showing and I couldn't let it pass without comment.

"Don't you think this divine force might be better employed stopping war or feeding starving people, rather than working to get you up to Scotland?"

Mike didn't know. Despite that, he cheerfully restated his belief.

"You've been put into my life to get me to the end of the Pennine Way. For the first few days I thought I'd have to cut it short, but now I've realised that at this rate we'll finish it in sixteen days. Then you'll go out of my life and I'll never see you again."

I started to realise why Mike had thought I might take offence when he first started explaining all this to me. He saw me as a pawn in a spiritual game of chess, a celestial tool, if you will. It occurred to me that I've been called a tool a few times in my life, but never quite so elegantly. I wasn't upset by it: Mike was an agreeable companion and I couldn't have found it in myself to get angry with him.

Of course, maybe the divine force had selected me for that reason.

We spent an entertaining couple of hours, verbally chasing each other around the debating table. Mike knew how he felt and that was all the "evidence" he needed. I put the view that an opinion does not have merit purely because someone holds it, that some sort of objective evidence is required. Merely *feeling* something to be true cannot, of itself, be sufficient evidence that it *is* true. In my assessment, mere feelings and personal comfort don't determine whether something is right or true. In Mikes view they very definitely do.

Maybe it says something for both of us that, at the end of the evening, we were still friends.

*****

The night was pitch black when we stepped back out of the pub and the wind was still blasting the campsite. We managed to find our tents in the gloom and settled ourselves in for the night, and for the coming storm.

We humans have become habituated to shelter, food and the company of other humans. Maybe it's because these are basic needs for us; maybe it's because these needs are essential for our survival and those humans well-suited to achieving them were best fitted to survive and pass on their genes. Whatever the reason, I know that if I had got straight into my tent when I arrived here, I'd have passed a fitful night. As it was, fortified by a good meal and the enjoyment of human company, warmed by my time in the pub, I slid into my sleeping bag, arranged my things into their night-time order and drifted off to sleep. The storm woke me twice in the night, but each time I simply checked that everything was as it should be, then turned over and went back to sleep.

Howling at the Moon

*****

I came to at 4.30 the next morning. I tried to turn over and resume sleeping, the approach that had worked so well for me in the night, but it wasn't to be. I had a quite insistent feeling that it was time to take a trip to the lavatory.

It was evident that the wind had dropped before I'd so much as opened the tent door. I pulled on my shoes and stepped outside into that muffled quiet that you only get with particularly thick fog. Like Wainwright all those years ago, although it was very close to me, I couldn't see the pub. I knew where it was though, ahead of me in the murk, so I set off towards the Toilet, Outside, Campers for the use of.

When I got back to my tent, I could see that Mike's tent was open. He was awake and studying the thick fog which swirled in spirals outside his front door.

We agreed to have breakfast straightaway and get moving, the alternative, trying to get warm and lying in the fog for another hour, being a much less attractive option.

Despite the cold wind, it was still foggy. I remembered that Wainwright had spent just an hour here in the middle of the day, but in similar conditions. The pub, he noted, was invisible by the time he had taken twenty paces away from it. Far be it from me to "black dog" a hiker as celebrated as Alfred Wainwright, but I reckon we'd lost the pub within ten paces.[4]

We were heading east-north-east across Sleightholme Moor. Our path took us downhill through bogs and wet feet were something of a shock that early in the morning, especially after a nice warm sleeping bag, but wet feet it was.

Our way was marked by a succession of white marker posts, each about four feet high. Like most things on the moors

---

[4] *Verb: to black dog someone. One-upmanship, e.g., "Nigel won't be outdone: if you've got a black dog, his dog's blacker."*

they were showing the ravages of time and weather, and most were faded and hard to pick out. Others were missing or leaning drunkenly to one side, a characteristic which reduced their height and made them harder to spot in the fog. We ended up walking along a compass bearing and treating the marker posts as occasional assistance rather than anything definitive.

Mike led, and I was doing quite well until I put my left foot on what looked like solid ground, only for it to plunge in up to the knee. I yelped and dropped to the ground as if I'd been shot.

Concerned by my shout, and the fact that I was lying in the bog, Mike came back and helped me to my feet. I brushed off those parts of the bog that hadn't soaked into my clothes and we carried on.

The murk surrounding us began to thin as we descended Sleightholme Moor and visibility increased around us. That wasn't as helpful as it sounds because the landscape was the same whichever direction we looked in. We were walking across peat bog: moss and heather under our feet, water everywhere. Overhead, the fog was such that I could look directly at the sun, a bright grey circle in the dark grey atmosphere. It was as if I was looking at it through ground glass.

By the time we reached Sleightholme Beck, the fog had opened up. The sky directly above us was bright blue with sunshine streaming through. In the distance, surrounding us on every horizon, the thick grey fog sat, immobile, like a disconsolate grey circle around us.

We crossed the River Greta by God's Bridge, Hillaby's "flat slab of limestone the size of a barn door," and ascended past the old lime kiln to the foot passage under the main A66 road.

There was no monument or sign, but both Mike and I knew that just after the A66, as we were crossing Deepdale, we would pass the halfway point of the Pennine Way. We both knew it but neither of us stopped or even mentioned it, we just kept walking.

As I walked, I fought back the growing feeling that I'd accomplished nothing. All that sweat and toil, all that pushing on tired legs and we'd only reached halfway! If the project had seemed huge when I'd started out at Edale, it felt even larger now. It was a depressing fact that the effort put in so far only served to emphasise the enormity of the undertaking. Then again, experience has taught me that a long walk *will* mess with your head. The trick is to anticipate the negative thoughts and, when they appear, to ruthlessly snap them off and carry on.

A little further on we stopped for a breather and I reached into the side pocket of my rucksack for my water bottle. The pocket was empty! Flustered by the absence of something which I usually keep in the same place, I checked the pocket on the other side. That contained my map, as it always does.

The presence of my map only served to confuse me further. If that was in place then all was well with the world and everything else should be in its place. I hurriedly took off my rucksack to check visually. Surely my water bottle would be where it always was? I'd merely missed it when I reached into the side pocket?

But the pocket was empty and the water bottle was gone.

I puzzled over where I could have lost it and realised quickly that it must have spilled out when I fell forward into the bog below the Tan Hill Inn. It was an emotional moment for me because the water bottle was a Father's Day present from my son and daughter many years ago. It had accompanied me on backpacking trips across England, Wales, Scotland and France. Even though the children had grown up and left home, and even though the metal bottle was battered and dented, I still used it on every trip. It was almost an article of faith.

For a moment, I thought about going back to look for it, but only for a moment because reality tempered that thought very quickly. It wasn't a practical proposition. The moors

The North Pennines

were big, we'd covered a lot of ground that morning and there was no guarantee that I could re-trace my steps exactly. I felt a lump in my throat. Maybe I was worn down from days of walking, but it's no exaggeration to say that, for a split second, I could have cried.

Mike asked what was up and I told him. He used a water bottle but also drank copious amounts of Coca Cola from plastic bottles, carrying the empties and throwing them away when we were in a town and he passed a bin. Ever practical, he gave me an empty Coke bottle and I washed it out in a stream and refilled it with water.

The Pennine Way took us around Blackton Reservoir and on the north side of it, Mike pointed out Hannah's Meadow.

Hannah's Meadow is now a Site of Special Scientific Interest. The farm, originally named Low Birk Hatt, was for decades the home of Miss Hannah Hauxwell who became well-known in the 1970s when a television documentary showed the harsh conditions in which she lived and farmed. Her income was about a tenth of the national average wage for the time and her life was one of unremitting hard work, not least because she carried on working the farm alone after her parents died, for many years without mains water or electricity. Hannah retired in 1988 and the sale of the farm provided her with funds for a retirement home in a nearby village.

The hedges were only just beginning to bud, but with the sun shining and the grass growing, it was hard to imagine what this place must be like in winter. A nearby noticeboard informed me of the Annual Cycle of Meadow Management:

Spring - Stock are removed from meadows to allow the hay crop to grow.

Summer – Hay crop cut in August followed by cows grazing the late grass.

Autumn – Sheep brought onto the meadows to run with

the tup in November before winter rest period.
Winter – Sheep lamb in the meadows followed by muck spreading.

It was meant to be an explanation but to my mind it provoked more questions than it answered. Where do the stock go when they are removed from the meadows in spring? Where have the cows been kept before they're put onto the late grass in August? Why do farmers breed sheep so that they lamb in the coldest, harshest time of the year?

I bet Hannah Hauxwell could have answered all those questions without even pausing for thought, and I suppose that just shows how remote we have become from the land and the sources of our food. Without intending to, I illustrated that fact by tearing the wrapper off a Snickers bar and eating it.

We walked along the side of Harter Fell and there was Middleton-in-Teesdale, ahead and below us. We strode over green turf, nibbled short by the sheep and dotted with taller clumps of wiry straw-coloured grass, the sort of stuff New Zealanders call tussock grass.

The campsite on the edge of town was a tidy affair, with a sheltered little camping patch tucked away behind the rows of caravans. It had trees on three sides of it, which gave it rather a woodland feel and it used to be the town's main railway station. The platforms and station buildings could clearly be made out amongst the caravans and mobile homes.

We paid in the campsite's reception area, where the lady we dealt with gently steered us towards the idea that it wasn't worth her while turning on the hot water in the campers' toilet block because it would cost her money and the water wouldn't warm up in time for us to use it.

I caught Mike's eye and he caught mine. We were both thinking the same thought: it was tempting to insist on hot water, but if we did, that insistence might incline her to decide the campsite wasn't open because of the hot water issue. We both kept schtum, paid the fee and then moaned like drains to each other as soon as we got outside.

An hour later, with my laundry done and my mind and body invigorated by a cold shower, I was ready to take on the fleshpots of Middleton.

Middleton-in-Teesdale is a pleasant little town: the sort of quiet, rural community you come away from and think about returning to. Something of the feel of it was just right.

Which shows you how a place can change. In 1938, Alfred Wainwright described it thus:

"Industry has, in fact, made a mess of this part of Teesdale ... They have cheerfully despoiled their natural surroundings so that money can be won from the earth, they have sacrificed a heritage of beauty and built a cinema."

We couldn't find the cinema, but Mike had a taste for fish and chips so we headed to the chippie. Inside, a sign happily proclaimed, "Everything fried in premium beef dripping." I spent half an hour in the company of, I think, the best cod and chips I have ever eaten, and then we stepped back outside and found ourselves a pub.

The walk out of Middleton the next morning was beautiful. We tramped along through woods carpeted with bluebells, a bright deep-blue haze stretching away from us. The dark skies began to open up and the Tees, on our right, looked majestic.

Whin Sill, the large igneous rock intrusion becomes very evident in Teesdale. This large band of dolerite is responsible for the waterfalls Low Force, High Force and Cauldron Snout, and for High Cup, over towards Dufton.

Low Force added to the beauty of the dale, as any waterfall would, and it served as an appetiser for its roaring big brother a little further upstream: High Force.

There is no longer any trace of Wainwright's "hideous lead mine" in the dale. AW was of the view that, "High Force deserves a poem, but it will never be written until the mine is abandoned and the railway torn up." Well, the mine was abandoned and the railway was torn up in the 1950s. Today, you'd have to look hard to find any trace of either. So, who will write that poem for Teesdale?

Not me. In spite of the landscape around me, I wasn't in a poetic frame of mind, so I pushed off, going further up Teesdale. The quarry on the far bank of the Tees is still active, and it gave some small impression of what this dale must have been like when it was still an industrial area, but on its own it was quickly passed.

Upper Teesdale is one of the most desolate parts of the Pennine Way. Seeming to consist mostly of smashed rock, fast flowing water and dark skies, it reminded me strongly of Iceland.

We rounded Falcon Clints, hopping from boulder to boulder on the eastern edge of the Tees. I knew what was coming next and the anticipation heightened because I could hear it before I could see it: Cauldron Snout.

Cauldron Snout, where the River Tees passes over the hard-rock dolerite steps of the Whin Sill, is reckoned to be the longest waterfall in England. Immediately above it is the dam which holds back Cow Green reservoir.

When John Hillaby passed through here in the 1960s, Cow Green was the subject of much controversy. Imperial Chemical Industries Limited had applied for permission to create a reservoir at Cow Green to supply water to their factories and chemical plants thirty miles downstream. The river downstream was heavily polluted and so useless for their purposes: the water would have to come from higher up the catchment area and a dammed reservoir would allow them to regulate the flow. The reservoir was to be formed by damming the River Tees above Cauldron Snout and flooding Cow Green, just to the north of the prospective dam.

The controversy came about because Cow Green contained rare species of tundra plants, some of them unique to the British Isles. In consequence, Hillaby notes, the Parliamentary bill proposing the dam "was opposed by every biologist of distinction in the country." That may have been so, but after a full Parliamentary debate the plan was approved and the reservoir constructed. It opened in 1971. Possibly the only long-term good to come out of this episode was a growing realisation that plants, like animals, needed statutory protection, a realisation that eventually culminated in the Wildlife and Countryside Act of 1981.

From Cow Green we started heading west along a stony track, hard underfoot, parallel with Maize Beck which flowed alongside but to the south of us. The grey ceiling overhead seemed to get lower as we plodded on underneath it.

The other side of Maize Beck was out of bounds, at least to the likes of Mike and I. Some 24,000 acres there are controlled by the Ministry of Defence, and they form the Warcop Training Area. This huge area of land was taken under military control in 1942 to train tank crews ahead of the D Day landings. So expansive is it that most of the armoured formations which took part in D Day trained here. Today, the area is an "all arms" training site and large *Danger* signs have been placed all along the northern boundary to warn walkers on the Pennine Way not to stray south. Disappointingly, the moors were quiet and there were no whizzes or bangs as we passed the ranges.

We started to skirt Dufton Fell and then dropped down to the edge of Maize Beck. My map showed our path crossing the beck, but there was no sign of a bridge on the map or on the ground. After much deliberation and careful selection, we found a rocky shelf where the beck got wider and, as a result, ran shallower, and we splashed our way across. Predictably, just around the next bend in the beck was a large footbridge.

Mike bent forward to flick some water-weed off his trousers and then straightened up. He pointed at the bridge and asked, in mock outrage, "What's your problem with using

109

that?"

I told Mike I had no problem with using the bridge and, to prove it, I jogged up to it and walked across it. Unfortunately that left me on the wrong side of the beck, so I had to turn round a bit sheepishly and walk back across the bridge again, all the while trying to look as if I'd meant to do that from the start.

Very soon we could see the land ahead dropping away from us. There was a near horizon which had an abrupt edge to it and, beyond that, a far distant horizon of lower, greyer hills. As we got closer, the deep glacial gorge of High Cup opened up before us.

High Cup is a text book U-shaped valley, the sheer size of which makes it difficult to take in. To stand there and see it all without moving your head seems impossible, as you notice one aspect of it here and then a different one there, and then another somewhere else. It's that splendid.

The wind stopped me from tarrying for too long. I took my camera out at High Cup Nick, the waterfall at the head of High Cup, but I didn't want to get too near the edge: I'm six foot one and fifteen stone, but the wind was so strong that I genuinely felt I might be blown over the side. Then the first drops of rain started to fall. I remembered the National Trails website had told me the path from Dufton to High Cup is "an old miner's track" and should only be undertaken in good weather. I didn't have time to hang about waiting for good weather. Anyway, I decided, if an old miner can walk it, I certainly should be able to.

The downhill stretch into Dufton felt like a long way, although in reality it was only a few kilometres. Dufton's only claim to fame is a fountain, which doesn't work, on the village green, but it's a pleasant little village even so. Mike and I set ourselves up at the campsite and booked a table for dinner at The Stag Inn.

That evening, we left The Stag tired but replete, which was about as good as we were going to get in the circumstances.

The North Pennines

Our campsite had devoted the most sheltered areas to camper vans and caravans, and the tent field was a small, more exposed area. We passed a cold, cold night. Morning found me mopping condensation out of the tent and wondering when summer was likely to arrive this far north.

We left Dufton through green fields and under bright blue skies. Between the fields were occasional woods, the trees covered in a slight green haze of very new buds, starting to break out despite the cold. Maybe summer was coming after all.

As we got higher up the lower slopes of Green Fell I could, if I turned, see the fells of the Lake District away in the west across the Eden Valley. I paused and looked at it. The last time I'd seen the Lake District from the east was when I'd walked the Coast to Coast Walk a few years before and the view before me was very similar. At that stage of the Coast to Coast, of course, I was only a few days into the walk. On my current walk, in contrast, I was well advanced. I'd almost reached the edge of my second map and after that I had only one map left to walk across.

At the top of Knock Old Man I found a flat stone and sat down by the rectangular cairn for a snack. It was still cold, despite the sunshine, but the clearer weather gave me long views away to the west. I could even see Mike behind me, still slogging up the rockfall on Green Fell. I dug into my pack and put on another layer of clothing, because I knew we'd sit here for a while longer after Mike eventually reached me.

I chatted with Mike when he arrived and sipped water while he ate and drank, then we got back to our feet, albeit with the air of people who could happily have sat down for the rest of the day. We were up high now, at 780m. My map showed a little more uphill and then some ups and downs until we reached Cross Fell, at 893m the highest point on the Pennine Way. Across to our left stood the massive golf-ball sphere of Great Dun Fell radar station and we set off towards it.

As we did so, we had the usual conversation which is common to all walkers: how far would we walk today and where would we stay tonight?

My original plan had been to stay at Greg's Hut, the bothy on the north side of Cross Fell, but we'd been making better time than I'd expected, so we'd arrive at the bothy earlier than I'd planned. It wouldn't hurt to take a little time out from walking, but we were in the wettest part of England: if the weather was fine, shouldn't we make the most of it and keep going?

If we did keep walking, where should we walk to? Garrigill was 10km after Greg's Hut and Alston was only another 8km after Garrigill. We decided to decide later.

It was a strange feeling, passing the radar station on the top of Great Dun Fell. This was a wild, lonely place, but the radar station was evidence not just of human activity but of the most technologically advanced type of human activity. However, the wire fence surrounding it and preventing access killed any fellow human feeling. We're here and you're there, it seemed to say, and don't ask if you can use our toilet because we'll only say no.

As I rounded the radar station I could see Cross Fell behind it. Over my right shoulder was a large bog that my map showed as the source of the River Tees and, away to the south-east of me, I could see the sun shimmering on the distant Cow Green Reservoir, the subject of all that controversy fifty years ago.

The climate up here is classed as "sub-arctic" and winter snow has been recorded as lying on Cross Fell as late as June. It used to be called Fiends' Fell in pagan times but, so the story goes, Saint Augustine drove out the evil spirits and erected a cross on the fell top to stop them returning.

We stopped in the stone windbreak on top of Cross Fell and Mike consulted his guidebook. This, he told me, was supposed to be the hardest day on the Pennine Way. We'd been lucky with the weather, but even so we'd covered a respectable distance so I think we were entitled to a little self-congratulation.

I didn't see a single fiend during our time on Cross Fell. Evidence, were evidence needed, that St Augustine did a thorough job all those years ago. Or should I have assumed the presence of fiends because there was no evidence that they *weren't* there? I decided not to mention fiends to Mike.

*****

From Cross Fell, the Pennine Way runs north-northwest and then makes a ninety degree turn to the right, towards Greg's Hut.

Greg's Hut is the only bothy on the Pennine Way, although there are two emergency huts up in the Cheviot Hills between Byrness and Kirk Yetholm. Originally a miners' shop serving and accommodating the miners who were working too far up the hill to travel to and from Garrigill each day, the building was a disused ruin for many years. In 1968 the 40 year old John Gregory (the "Greg" of Greg's Hut) was killed in a climbing accident in the Alps. His parents funded the restoration of the building as a bothy and his friends provided the workforce to carry out the necessary repairs and maintenance. It still stands and is still kept up as a memorial to him. What a lovely memorial that is such a practical help to others!

It was 1.30 when Mike and I arrived at Greg's Hut. The weather couldn't have been better for walking and so this wasn't the day to rest up indoors. It was obvious to both of us that we had to continue at least as far as Garrigill.

The stretch to Garrigill was downhill, but long and surprisingly stony underfoot. By the time we reached the village we were footsore and the remaining miles to Alston were not attractive to us. Add to that the first sign of civilisation we saw in Garrigill: the George and Dragon, and the die was cast.

We paused outside the George and Dragon to debate whether or not we should sample their hospitality before finding the campsite. This was an exchange we had developed over many days and many pubs. It was more a formality than anything else, because we both knew we would sit outside the pub with a drink in the sunshine for a while, but it had become important that the correct form was followed. It was almost like a masonic ritual: one of us would suggest a brief pint and the other would agree. The first person would then backtrack a little and wonder out loud whether we should put the tents up first and the other would reply in the negative, asserting that we should make the most of the sunshine while we still had it. The Junior Deacon would ask if it was his round and the Senior Warden would respond no, it was his and did his colleague want crisps? It was all very pleasant.

At which point, one of the all-day drinkers who was seated on one of the two benches on the pavement outside the pub drew attention the disparity in size between our rucksacks by loudly enquiring why I was making the old bastard carry all the gear.

Mike went in to get the drinks while I expounded the benefits of not carrying a heavy load when backpacking, something I would have thought was self-evident but which I find myself explaining again and again. The name Alfred Wainwright carries a lot of weight in British walking circles, so I'll let him have the last say on the subject and then I'll shut up:

"How some hikers can enjoy themselves beneath the weight of their huge, fifty-pound burdens completely passes my comprehension."

And mine, AW, and mine.

Our next priority was accommodation or, more

accurately, somewhere flat and sheltered where we could assemble our own accommodation.

I had done my research before this hike and I knew that camping was permitted at Garrigill Village Hall, provided you phoned "Emily" first. Since neither of us could get a mobile phone signal in Garrigill, phoning Emily was a bit of a non-starter, so we wandered on from the George and Dragon, found the village hall and looked it over. A notice outside the hall stated that would-be campers or people wishing to use the bunkhouse should contact Emily and helpfully gave her address, the name of a house which I'd noticed as we passed it a minute or so ago.

"Or people wishing to use the bunkhouse". I read that bit again, this time out loud, just to make sure Mike hadn't missed it. He nodded sagely and added his thoughts.

"It might be easier to do some washing and get it dry if we were indoors."

I left Mike outside the village hall and crossed the quiet road back to Emily's house. She was next door, in the garden with her neighbour and what looked like someone's grandchildren. I asked about the bunkhouse and the neighbour accompanied me back to the hall, showed Mike and I the ropes and took a nominal fee from us.

Shoes off, we stretched out on our bunk-beds and planned the evening. Firstly, that all important cup of tea, we decided. Then showers, followed by laundry, then dinner in the pub. It was a masterplan, worthy of a top general, and we lost no time in putting it into effect.

The George and Dragon stuffed us with food, bless them, for we needed every calorie they had. It wasn't a late night for us, but by the time we got back to our bunks, our laundry was dry in the drying room. We were clean and fed, with 285km behind us; well set up for the remaining 138km of the Pennine Way.

*****

John Hillaby exhorted his readers to ignore the official route of the Pennine Way out of Garrigill. It was, he said, "hopelessly complicated", and he recommended walkers go due north to Alston, "the way the legions went".

This was confusing stuff, because the official route of the Pennine Way between Garrigill and Alston is about as straightforward as you can get. It runs along the south bank of the River South Tyne for a bit, following it closely, then crosses the river and sticks to the north bank, again following it closely. Maybe it took them a while to agree and implement this part of the Pennine Way route I mused, as I walked beside the river. Maybe in Hillaby's day, when the Pennine Way was just an infant, there might still have been a few rights of way issues or a few arguments about the route that they hadn't quite resolved.

Whatever the reasons for the disparity, the current route is a corker. In the valley of the South Tyne, the Pennine Way passes between hills, green slopes sweeping up and away on either side, the shadows of dry-stone walls showing as long, black lines across the landscape. Even in sunshine, though, it doesn't take much imagination to see how this countryside could transform into a harsh environment and how the scattered farms could quickly become isolated, when the snow comes.

It didn't take us long to reach Alston, "the highest market town in England, but otherwise unremarkable"[5], and we re-supplied at the grocery shop. It was still early and the prospect of a second breakfast, which had started as the mere germ of an idea in one of the recesses of my mind, quickly sprouted and grew until it became all-enveloping. Mike was of the same inclination so we started prowling the streets of Alston, looking for a supplier to meet our need.

Our optimism was ill-founded, for we were looking for

---

[5] *John Hillaby again.*

a food establishment, open and serving, in a small, remote English town at nine o'clock on a Sunday morning. I found myself charging up to premises which looked as if they served food only to get close and find that they didn't or, even worse, that they did but not at nine o'clock on a Sunday. The more I was rebuffed, the more precise my craving became. I'd started out with the vague idea of finding somewhere "for breakfast", but after twenty minutes of trying café door handles, checking side streets for likely premises and an embarrassing incident at a ladies' hairdresser, I knew with great clarity that I wanted a full English cooked breakfast with a large mug of tea, and with toast and marmalade to follow.

It wasn't to be. Realisation dawned slowly, but gradually grew until it smothered the very concept of breakfast. I was disappointed, but not, I told myself, because Alston had failed to provide me with breakfast. I was disappointed because I had allowed my craving to run riot without first checking that it was even possible. Best just to move on, I decided. Forget the whole thing.

Mike and I intended to follow the railway out of Alston, so we headed for the station.

Alston Station was a pretty place, although I couldn't help thinking that it might not have looked as spick and span when it served a working industrial railway.

The Alston branch line was built to connect the lead mines around Alston with the main Newcastle and Carlisle Railway at Haltwhistle. Work started on the line in 1850 and it was opened in 1852. By the 1960s, traffic on the line was down and it was recommended for closure, however the lack of an all-weather road alternative delayed closure for another decade and the Alston branch line eventually shut in 1976 (and that fact alone reinforces how inhospitable it can be up in the north Pennines in winter). Today the South Tynedale Railway, as it's now known, is run as a heritage railway by a charity.

Mike and I had a nose around the station buildings. It

was too early to expect signs of life but, we felt, you never know. At the very least the toilets might be unlocked.

I was standing looking at a spectacularly clean and shiny steam locomotive, which looked strangely dormant without smoke or steam coming from it, when I saw Mike further up the platform beckoning me with to join him, with a strangely conspiratorial air. I abandoned the loco and strolled along the platform to meet him. He pointed at a door in front of him, which opened into one of the station buildings.

"Look – I've found a café."

And he had.

This part of the old railway station had been converted into a small café. The lights were on and we could see someone moving about inside. The chairs were still on the tables, put there to facilitate cleaning the evening before, but this place was clearly in business.

I tried the door-handle and the door opened. The café was open!

We stepped inside and were greeted by a cheerful lady who seemed to be re-organising a complicated array of cooking implements behind the serving counter. She asked what she could get us.

Chastened by our experiences in the centre of Alston just a short while ago, we asked her what she had. She replied by passing us two menus.

"Anything on there."

A few minutes later I was sitting opposite Mike eating a large cooked breakfast. We'd taken the chairs down while our hostess prepared our orders and by the time we'd finished setting the place up for the day, our food was ready.

We took our time over mugs of tea, enjoying our conversation with the lady manager, and it was with genuine regret that we finally got up to leave. I stepped back out onto the platform and Mike pulled the door closed behind us. I turned to check he was with me.

"Wow," he said, "She did us a big favour."

I didn't see it.

"How do you mean?"

Mike pointed to the sign behind the glass door he'd just closed.

"The place doesn't open for another hour."

I leaned toward the door and scanned the sign. He was quite right.

We set off down the platform, praising the kindness of strangers.

*****

The Pennine Way skips about a bit after Alston, but the walk along the railway is beautiful.

We soon saw the old station sign and the old platform at Slaggyford. Alfred Wainwright reached here in 1938, hiking the other way, towards Alston. He was behind schedule and needed food but there was no pub or other place of refreshment in Slaggyford. Undaunted, AW bought a stamp in the Post Office as a conversation opener and asked where he might get a meal. They referred him to the house of an elderly lady in the village. She gave him dinner and he records her embarrassment at having to ask him for payment. She asked for a shilling[6]: Wainwright gallantly paid more.

In twenty-first century Slaggyford there is no Post Office in which to buy a stamp or ask where you can get a meal. I speculated about the reception I might get, were I to knock on someone's door and ask.

Above Slaggyford we passed Hartleyburn Common, an area that will soon look very different now that an application for an open cast mine has been approved. They reckon about 140,000 tonnes of coal will be extracted around the village of

---

[6] *One shilling (written 1/-) = 5p in modern money.*

Halton Lea Gate, a topic which, I should imagine, must have enlivened parish council meetings considerably over the last few years. I wondered what AW would have thought about it all.

Chapter 8

Northumberland

Hadrian's Wall: milecastles and Mithraism. – North of the wall, into Northumberland. – Trail magic. – Bellingham with a "j". – The Story of the Long Pack. – The Cheviot Hills and the border fence. – Kirk Yetholm.

We approached Hadrian's Wall by marching up the road to it, just as the legions must have done. Mike declared the morning "a once in a century day," and I had to agree with him. It was a bright, clear morning; blue skies arching overhead and hardly a cloud in the world, just the gossamer-cobweb strands of fine, high-level cirrus clouds. The sunshine was defining the landscape by the dark, impenetrable shadows which resulted from it anywhere there was an undulation in the ground or a structure upon it.

I'd encountered the Hadrian's Wall before, but it was just as impressive when I saw it again, its serenity and its majesty contributing much to its impact. I remembered writer Ronald Turnbull's description of how he climbed over a stile to leave a wood and found Hadrian's Wall in front of him:

"I went back into the wood and had a sandwich, just so as to step over that stile a second time."

At last, here was a landmark worthy of our journey! "Get to the wall," I'd said to myself before I left home, "and it's almost done."

Now I was at the wall, I could see that it wasn't almost done. Nowhere near, in fact. I was still on the second of a set of three maps covering the Pennine Way and I still had a hundred kilometres to walk. Nevertheless, reaching the wall was such a significant milestone that the achievement of it buoyed me up more than I was pulled down by the realisation of how much was left. I wasn't daunted. What was a hundred kilometres? Four days, and four not-too-hard days at that.

What stands out about Hadrian's Wall to the casual observer is its close adherence to the shape of the land. The Roman surveyors utilised every advantage there was to be had from the geography. The wall's exact purpose is still debated, but whether it was defensive or whether it was built to control movement (and maybe, thus, to collect taxes), it is an imposing, controlling feature.

There was a lot of up and down as we progressed along the Hadrian's Wall section of the Pennine Way, but it was such a beautiful morning and such an iconic location that I could have walked it all day. I knew it would be a wrench to leave it behind when we arrived at Housesteads Fort.

Many interesting finds have been made along the wall and some of the most interesting are at Housesteads. In 1822 an excavation here discovered a Mithraic temple. Mithraism was a cult much in favour with Roman army officers. The cult had started in Persia and spread across the Roman Empire. Mithras, a god born from a rock, was eternally at war with evil. The legend says that he captured a bull and killed it in a cave in order to release its power to benefit mankind. Mithraic temples tended to be small and underground, to remind adherents of the cave where Mithras slew the bull. Devotees went through seven complicated grades of initiation and knew one another by a secret handshake. The general consensus seems to be that Mithraism was exterminated by early Christians.

Mike and I turned left at Housesteads and headed north across farmland.

Years ago I'd backpacked along Hadrian's Wall with friends. New to this part of the country, I remember standing by the wall and looking out across Northumberland to the north. What would it be like to walk out there, I'd wondered, out in that vast empty wilderness, beyond the bounds of civilisation as defined by the wall? Now, I was to find out.

*****

We passed the old lime kilns on Ridley Common, standing stark in the middle of nowhere. Most old lime kilns that I've passed on my travels seem to be near some form of transport, like a canal or a railway line so that the raw materials and the finished product can be easily transported. On Ridley Common, there was nothing. How did they get the limestone and the firewood to the kilns, I wondered? I could see no clue, leading me by a process of exclusion to conclude that horse and cart can have been the only method. Presumably the lime produced by the kilns must have been applied to the fields immediately surrounding them. The lime must have generated a decent improvement in crop yields to make all that effort worthwhile.

Within a few minutes the wall was out of sight and but a distant memory. Within a couple of hours I'd walked through forests and across bogs, and I'd come to the conclusion that this section of the Pennine Way is dull and drab without, my journal notes, a single redeeming feature. I was beginning to realise why Wainwright thought the Pennine Way should finish at Hadrian's Wall. John Hillaby summed up this part of Northumberland best: "a close-planted arboreal slum."

The dense conifer tree-farms and the bogs gave way to fields and bogs, and then the path dropped down a steep slope to cross Warks Burn before climbing back up an even steeper slope on the opposite side. At the top was a handwritten sign promising "trail magic" at the next farm.

"Trail magic" is an unexpected act of kindness, usually involving food, drink or transport, given to hikers. Although trail magic happens a lot on the long trails in the USA, this was the first time I had seen anything like it in England. That fact alone made it worthwhile to make a stop at Horneystead Farm.

On the farm, more signs directed us to an outhouse. We paused in front of the farm yard. On one side of the yard a chained-up dog barked so overenthusiastically that he seemed to border on some type of canine derangement. I carefully skirted the dog, hoping that his chain and the chain's wall attachment would hold, and opened the outhouse door. Inside I found a well-stocked fridge, a kettle, a sofa and all manner of things useful to hikers. On the wall was a sign that explained what this was all about:

My mother started doing teas at Horneystead to Pennine Way walkers in 1980. She enjoyed meeting people, and amazingly some 'do it again' walkers remember her and, at times, pretty hard rock buns!

We moved here in 1996 and felt we didn't have the time to actually be here and serve teas.

However in 2007 we completed the P.C.T. – Pacific Crest Trail in America (if anyone wants to experience 5-6 months of the most incredible scenery, wilderness and exhilaration, please, take some time off work and do it!) We experienced the most amazing kindness by the people out there who lived near the trail that we were determined to do our bit for fellow walkers! So enjoy and <u>happy walking.</u>

I boiled the kettle and made a cup of tea, Mike took a cold drink from the fridge. We sat outside and chatted with each other as if there was no dog barking incessantly and throwing itself towards us to test its chain. It was a most welcome break, if you were able to ignore the dog.

Reinvigorated as much by the random kindness of strangers as we were by the rest and the drinks, we were soon crushing the miles again. Pausing only briefly to grin at the sign for Shitlington (I think I've already mentioned my sense of humour issues), we quickly found ourselves on the edge of Bellingham (pronounced "Bell-in-jum").

Bellingham is a lovely little stone-built border town and nowadays you'd never know that for many centuries it was defined by its close proximity to the Scottish border. In more recent times, John Hillaby noted, "The English seem completely indifferent to the boundary and all that it used to mean. But on the other side of the border, they are a bit more touchy."

A touchiness which seems to have culminated in a full-blown independence movement. And they weren't the only ones getting touchy. Mike had started to look queasy as we passed through the last section of bogs and here in Bellingham he announced his intention to book into a hotel for the night because he felt ill. We quickly established that there was nothing I could do for him. To be honest, I wasn't completely surprised: I'm OK for a bit of First Aid, but if I'd been ill the last thing I would have wanted was me providing the nursing.

We both needed the town centre, so I paused and asked a local elder the quickest way to get to it. I was treated to a long ramble about going down side-streets, across a bridge, through ginnels and round corners, all in a thick local accent. Starting to feel that life was passing me by and wondering if he was going to reach the end of his monologue before one of us died, I interrupted to say that I'd seen a sign a while back telling me to simply turn right at Lloyd's Bank and the campsite was 75m on. At which point he replied, in perfect English, "Oh yes, you could do that instead."

I was about to ask him, 1) if it wasn't too much trouble, would he be kind enough to tell us how we might find Lloyd's

Bank, and, 2) if he had trained at the same village idiot school as the clown from Cowling[7], when I felt Mike's hand on my elbow and we moved on.

In the town centre, Mike booked into The Cheviot Hotel and went to telephone his wife. We agreed to meet there later for dinner but I wondered, as I walked away, whether he would be well enough to carry on by the time I re-joined him. Talking with his wife might fortify him for the rest of the walk or it might remind him of the many comforts available at home, which can be, of course, very tempting when you don't feel well. Mike and I had a symbiotic relationship and we'd helped each other extensively along the Pennine Way. I hoped I wouldn't lose him for the last few days.

Away to my right, as I wandered back out of The Cheviot Hotel, was St Cuthbert's Church. St Cuthbert's is known for a particular grave in its churchyard and for the tale that goes with it: the story of the long pack.

In 1723, so the story goes, one Colonel Ridley, recently retired from the East India Company with a fortune, left his house, Lee Hall in Bellingham, to winter with his family in London. He left three servants to look after the house and grounds: Alice, Richard and Edward.

While Colonel Ridley and his family were away a pedlar called at the house. Pedlars were usually welcomed because they brought a range of goods not easily acquired locally and, of course, gossip and news from all the towns and villages they'd passed through. This pedlar had a particularly large pack because he had just bought new stock, and Alice gave him a meal.

After eating, the pedlar asked for lodging for the night. Alice was unable to authorise this in her master's absence and she refused. The pedlar complained that he couldn't carry such a large pack any further. After some discussion it was agreed

---

[7] *See pages 67-68.*

that he would leave it at Lee Hall, find accommodation elsewhere and call for it the next day as he recommenced his round.

After the pedlar had gone, Alice thought she saw the pack move. She cried out, and Richard and Edward ran into the house, Edward with a gun he had been using to scare birds on the estate.

Edward fired at the pack and blood poured from it. Inside was a man, now dead, with a cutlass tied to his wrist, four loaded pistols and a whistle.

It was evident that the plan was for the man in the pack to free himself during the night and admit his partner-in-crime, the "pedlar", so that they might burgle the house together.

Fearing that the pedlar and his associates would be likely to attack the house later that night, expecting to be let in by the man in the pack, the servants called on neighbours who had access to firearms for support. When the attack came in the night, there were enough people in Lee Hall armed with guns to repel it. Several of the attackers were unhorsed by the gunfire from the hall, but no-one would leave the building to check on them in the dark.

The attackers removed the bodies of their shot colleagues under cover of darkness and the corpse inside the long pack was never claimed, so no-one involved in the crime was ever identified.

Lee Hall still stands, south-east of Bellingham next to the River North Tyne. Richard remained in service to the Ridley family for the rest of his life, on a good salary. Edward joined an infantry regiment and was shot through the shoulder at the battle of Fontenoy in 1745. He survived and retired to take a farm in Scotland. Alice married a tobacconist in Hexham. The unidentified body of the pedlar's accomplice in the long pack was buried in St Cuthbert's churchyard in Bellingham.

Howling at the Moon

*****

I was back at The Cheviot Hotel at the appointed hour, but it was quite a while before Mike showed up. I got him a drink and we sat opposite each other at a small table. You wouldn't have looked at him and said, "Here's a bloke who's going to breeze the next 66km of bogs and hills," but he did look a little better than he had when I'd left him a few hours earlier. I was relieved when he told me he was fit enough to continue the walk.

The next morning we met on time in the centre of the village, then set off up the steep hill out of town that constituted the first part of that day's walk. It was, according to Mike's landlord of last night, the easiest day's walking on the whole Pennine Way.

Of course, any day can be the easiest day's walking; it all depends on how you plan your days. Then again, the confident, unbiased assertion of someone with a heavy investment in the tourist trade was enough to make us feel confident about the day ahead of us. And after that, there would only be two days left.

The steep hill out of Bellingham gave onto moorland and, in its turn, the moorland gave way to forest.

Not much of the Pennine Way is forested. I'd been walking across moors for almost two weeks and I was looking forward to some woodland: leaf mould underfoot, sunlight filtering through the leafy canopy, that sort of thing. I quickly discovered I'd have to wait a bit longer.

We were entering Redesdale Forest, part of the much larger Kielder Forest. Kielder Forest covers 650km^2 which makes it one of the largest human-made forests in Europe. The forest was planted in the 1920s and 1930s using a labour-force drawn from the unemployed, so the forest served a dual purpose: it provided a national timber reserve to make up the stock depleted by the First World War and it provided employment during a period when work was much needed.

I usually enjoy walking through woodland, but here I couldn't shake off the impression that I was hiking through a vast tree farm. Monoculture seemed to be the order of the day, mile after mile of Sitka spruce. The tracks through the forest weren't the ancient woodland trackways of southern Britain, nor the old packhorse routes or drovers' trails so enjoyable to walk along in other places. These were long, wide heavy-vehicle tracks, tonnes of scalpings road-rollered into place so that the support vehicles of modern forestry can get in and out quickly and efficiently. There were few clearings and those that did exist were too rough to put a tent on if we'd needed to. Almost all of it seemed to be swimming in water, a vast forest in a bog. And that was just the wooded parts: the felled areas looked absolutely desolate, like some sad parody of a ghastly First World War battlefield.

I can't speak for the whole of Kielder Forest because I saw only a small part of it, but the part I saw was dismal, drab and boring. I suspected it could only have been made this way because the area is so sparsely populated and there must have been very few people around to object. The mission statement of the founders of Kielder Forest seems to have been, "It doesn't matter, no-one's going to see it." I hoped the next few days over the Cheviots would be better.

We were still in the forest when we passed the hamlets of Cottonshopeburnfoot and Blakehopeburnhaugh. These two tiny villages claim to have the longest place names in England, a fact which makes me think that not much happens up here.

Byrness, our stopping place that night, is mostly a collection of former forestry workers' houses dating from the 1930s. Some of these houses have been converted into the Forest View Inn and all I can say is, if there's a warmer welcome anywhere along the Pennine Way, then I'd like to hear about it. Mike and I took the weight off our feet in the lounge and within a minute, cups of tea were provided and our shoes were being cleaned for us. We chatted with other walkers and drank our tea. Then, in our own good time, we stirred our weary limbs and went to get cleaned up. I don't like to get over-confident because there are a lot of things that can go wrong on a long-distance walk, but I reckoned we were going to finish this one. I phoned a pub in Kirk Yetholm and booked a room for our last night.

Mike and I were in good spirits when we set out next morning. Even rolling grey clouds and a forecast of bad weather didn't dampen our spirits.

The first mile or so out of Byrness was a steep climb but we were soon above the forest, with views opening out all around. Below and behind us was Catcleugh Reservoir, ahead and to the sides the hills rolled off into the distance, a stormy sea of rough grassland, topped with a glowering grey sky.

A sign solemnly informed us:

You are now on the final 39km (24 miles) of the Pennine Way. In about 5km (3 miles) you will join the border ridge which climbs to its highest point at 815m (2674 ft) on The Cheviot. The landscape further north becomes a high plateau of volcanic lavas weathered over millions of years into domed hills. You have a few steep climbs ahead of you!

We quickly reached the border fence and stepped through into Scotland. Here was a landmark! Like Hadrian's Wall, this was a monumental point on our journey, made even more significant by the effort required to gain it! The fence consisted of nothing more than a few spindly strands of wire strung between elderly fence-posts. It looked indistinguishable from any other farm fence, but we recognised it for what it was and we grinned at each other like schoolboys.

We passed back into England and through the old Roman Camp at Chew Green, the outline of it still clearly visible on the ground. There was no other sign of humanity in any direction.

The mountain refuge hut, slightly south-west of Lamb Hill, proved to be just that and no more. If you've ever stopped in a bothy in the UK or a refuge in the Alps, you'll probably have a mental picture of cosiness and hospitality. None of that self-indulgent nonsense here! The hut was weatherproof and that's about all that could be said for it. With no sleeping platform and little floor space, it seemed to have been deliberately designed to render an overnight stay uncomfortable. You would only ever spend a night here, I reflected, if the alternative option of spending it outside was even worse. I get their thinking: clearly, the idea was to provide an emergency refuge, not a holiday chalet.

Our day ended at Russell's Cairn on Windy Gyle. Russell's Cairn is a 2m high pile of rock fragments and it is supposed to mark the spot where the English Lord Francis Russell died in 1585 at a truce meeting with the Scots. It seems that Russell was either murdered by the Scots or, depending on which version of the story you believe, by his own side in order to frame the Scots for the murder. Modern antiquarians think the cairn dates from the Bronze Age, but if it wasn't built to commemorate Russell, it does seem to have been named for him.

Mike and I had spent the day "slackpacking". Rather than camp in this high, weather-afflicted spot, we had arranged for transport to meet us and take us back to the Forest Inn in Byrness. Next morning we would be dropped back in the middle of nowhere and we would slog back up to Russell's Cairn and resume our walk from where we had left off. An unexpected bonus was that we had been able to leave our tents and sleeping bags in Byrness, thus carrying lighter packs for today only. The downside of this was, for the first time on this hike, we had no shelter with us and no provision for one should an emergency occur.

It was a long, steep slog downhill to the agreed pick up

Howling at the Moon

point, and it seemed a mere matter of minutes before we were being dropped back there with good wishes the next morning.

This was to be our final day on the Pennine Way, so we picked our way back up the old Roman road to Windy Gyle and Russell's Cairn. Yesterday's low, rolling grey cloud, under which I could see for miles, had been replaced by a thick fog with a visibility of about 20m at best.

If yesterday had reminded me how big and empty this part of the country is, today reminded me that I really didn't want to get lost in it. England has a higher population density than India[8] however, as we'd been told the night before by our landlady, in this part of Northumberland there are only 127 people living in 800 square miles. If we got lost, we'd probably stay lost for quite some time.

We were in good spirits, despite the fog. Mike convinced me that we had now finished the walk.

"If anything goes wrong today," he explained, "We'll still have to walk to Kirk Yetholm. So, whatever happens, we've finished the Pennine Way."

As the mist began to lift, I have to say it didn't feel like we'd finished. I could see an awful lot of the Cheviot Hills still to be crossed before we could reach Kirk Yetholm.

It will be interesting to see Kirk Yetholm, I thought to myself as I paced along the border ridge, trying to stay out of the swampy bits. Up until today it had been just a name, but we had expended so much effort and time to get to it.

Our path was not very clear and we had to pause on several occasions to consult my map and compass, and Mike's guidebook. I was surprised that there wasn't a more obvious tread and I said so. Mike showed me a comment in his guidebook: the Pennine Way is not as distinct in the Cheviots

---

[8] *England has a population density 413 people/km^2 (UK Office for National Statistics), India has 398 people/km^2 (UN Dept of Economic and Social Affairs).*

as it is in the Peak District because fewer walkers make it this far. Quite simply, so many people have dropped out by this stage that the path up here doesn't get the wear that it does down south. I wondered how the other walkers we'd camped with back at The Carriage House were getting on. Judith and Nigel, where were they? Still on the Pennine Way, or had they been forced home?

The weather forecast for the morning was for heavy rain, but neither Mike nor I were daunted by that: we were very close to completing the Pennine Way without experiencing a single drop of rain in the daytime, which must be some sort of record. The weather could do what it liked on our last day. As Mike said, we would walk to Kirk Yetholm whatever.

By now the fog had disappeared and thick, dark clouds raced and swirled overhead. The black sky seemed to be lowering itself down onto us, but without the fog visibility was restored and our route wasn't too difficult to find, so we made good time. Or maybe we were spurred on by the closeness of our destination?

We ignored the spur path which takes walkers up to the top of The Cheviot. Although it's the highest hill in this range at 815m, The Cheviot looked indistinguishable from all the other Cheviots. In any case, as I said to Mike, it would have been improvident to have climbed it on this trip: there are only a finite number of hills and they have to last us a lifetime.

We passed the Hen Hole, a deep glacial cut in the hillside and supposedly the haunt of fairies. Many years ago, the fairies are said to have lured a hunting party into the Hen Hole by their music, and the huntsmen were never able to find their way back out.

The mountain refuge hut near the Hen Hole is a twin of its colleague near Lamb Hill. It was empty, so Mike and I stepped in out of the wind and made a quick cup of tea. Named the Stuart Lancaster Memorial Hut, this hut is named after a walker who died in a snowstorm near here, a sad reminder of what can happen in these hills.

Our route out of the hills involved an ascent up The Schill (605m) and back down the other side, then we had a choice for our hike down into Kirk Yetholm: we could stay in England until the last minute and then drop down into Scotland, or we could turn into Scotland sooner and take a slightly lower route to KY, as I'd started referring to it. Mike and I spoke about it over our tea and decided upon the lower route. We were both, by now, very focussed on our journey's end.

As we started up The Schill there was a slight patter of rain and then the heavens opened. We quickly donned waterproofs, with hardly a pause, and strode on. I was in front and as I crested The Schill, passing through the great shattered rocks, it occurred to me that it was all downhill from that point to Kirk Yetholm.

I once knew a man who kept greyhounds. When they raced, he summarised their speed and concentration, and their physical action, with the phrase, "Head down, arse up", and that's how I felt as I flew down the hillside towards our destination. I waited several times for Mike to catch me up, but each time he did I shot off again down the hill.

After a couple of hours, the rain stopped. Mike caught up, took his spectacles off to wipe them and looked at me.

"We can't complain. Only two hours of rain in sixteen days."

I agreed. By this stage, I couldn't have cared less about the weather, but I had to admit we'd done well. The area through which the Pennine Way passes has twice the average rainfall for the United Kingdom, so Mike was right: we couldn't moan.

We hit a stretch of tarmac which formed a service road for a few small holiday chalets, and paced alongside Halter Burn, patches of gorse flashing bright yellow, the first bright colour we'd seen in the landscape for several days. Piles of river gravel and occasional engineering work showed what this little burn was capable of when in spate. Behind us, the domes of the Cheviots clustered together as if talking about us behind our backs; ahead of us, the valley opened out into Scottish farmland, neatly kept and well looked after.

Our road turned left onto a lane towards KY. I don't know why, but for some reason I'd expected to walk straight off the hill and into the village. A road with cars on jarred me somewhat.

I waited once again for Mike to catch up, for I was determined that we would walk the walk into the village side-by-side, and we did.

There was no-one about as we walked through Kirk Yetholm. The Pennine Way ends at a pub called The Border Hotel, so Mike and I shook hands outside the pub and then went in.

Inside were a couple of all-day drinkers avidly concentrating on daytime "reality" television, and a dog curled up under a "no dogs" sign. Wainwright was right: there was no fanfare, no brass band. No-one cared that we'd just walked from Edale and why should they? They see it every day, if they can look away from the telly.

Mike bought me a pint and we sat for a moment, each of us in quiet contemplation of his journey. I thought of how I'd come to start out on this walk, and about what I'd accomplished. My summary looked like this:

Kilometres walked:	*423*
Days walked:	*15.25*
Kilograms carried:	*6*
Photographs taken:	*437*
Moons howled at:	*0*

Part 2

Chapter 9

Trail Facts

The following is taken from an old and battered notice, undated, which can be found inside the mountain refuge hut near Lamb Hill in the Cheviots. It provides some interesting facts about the Pennine Way:

The Pennine Way was the first UK Long Distance Path (now National Trail) and was officially opened in 1965.

Its original theme was the provision of the opportunity to make long distance journeys through predominantly wild country. The ability to navigate by map and compass was and is intended to be a necessary skill for those undertaking the route.

The Pennine Way is 463km (289 miles) in total, including loops. It runs between Edale in Derbyshire and Kirk Yetholm in the Scottish borders taking in Northern England's finest moorland scenery and major scenic attractions. A full length walker would complete 429km (268 miles) by the recommended route.

The Trail has 319km of Public Footpath, 112km of Public Bridleway and 32km of Public Highway. 45km of the route is subject to alignment procedures. There are 535 access points to the Pennine Way from other Public Rights of Way and permissive paths.

The Pennine Way has an aggregate use of between 240,000 and 360,000 per annum. On the Pennine Way the vast majority of users are walkers. Most are daywalkers with around 10,000 long distance walkers although the balance in walker days is roughly 60/40.

Half the Pennine Way passes over open moorland, one quarter through rough grazing and only a tenth through forest and woodland or along riverbanks.

A long distance walker would complete 284km on gentle slopes of less than five degrees, 32km on slopes of ten to fifteen degrees and only 6km on steep slopes of more than fifteen degrees.

The average width of the Pennine Way is 2.85m. In 1989 this was 4.52m. Where new paths have been built the width was 11.1m in 1989 and only 1.6m on average in 1994.

The Pennine Way passes through three National Parks and one Area of Outstanding Natural Beauty. In all 365km of the route is in these designated areas. The Trail passes through two Environmentally Sensitive Areas (125km), 20 SSSIs and 2 NNRs (197km) and a World Heritage Site (16km).

In 1994 the Trail showed 24% light tramping impacts, 17% medium impacts and 13% heavy and extensive impacts. 46% of the trail is on manmade surfaces, 95% of which are in satisfactory or better condition.

There are 287 gates, 249 timber stiles, 183 stone stiles, and 204 bridges in a total of 1331 items of countryside furniture. Of these 78% are in satisfactory or better condition.

There are 458 signs and waymarks on the route 95% of which are in satisfactory or better condition. 43% include the Acorn symbol.

Services within 45 mins walk of the route provide 87 shops, 110 pubs, 23 cafés and tea shops, 49 public telephones and 17 information centres.

There are 8 railway stations, 50 points of access to bus services. Car access is catered for by 35 managed car parks and 53 locations where roadside parking is available.

Trail Facts

There are 208 providers of accommodation within 2km of the route, 133 Bed & Breakfast establishments, 46 Camping sites, 17 Hostels, and 12 Bunkbarns. In all these can provide up to 3554 bedspaces. 61% of accommodation costs less than £15 per person per night, and only 8% costs more than £20 per person per night.

Walker surveys indicate that 16% were walking less than two miles, 45% out for less than a full day, 32% for a full day walk, and 7% long distance walkers. Almost 30% were on a day trip and 68% on holiday or a short break.

The "average" long distance walker is male and between 16 and 44 years old. However, the overall balance is 60/40 male to female and almost 10% of walkers on Kinder are over 60.

45% of walkers came from Yorkshire, the North-west or Northern England, 13% from the East Midlands and 18% from the South-east. In total, 4% were not U.K. residents although 27% of walkers on the Hadrian's Wall section were of non U.K. origin.

22% of walkers stayed on the route, 24% travelled less than 10 miles to the start point of their walk, 24% 26-50 miles and 14% over 50 miles.

A sign at Grassholme Reservoir offers useful advice to anyone planning this walk:

Conditions in the Pennines can be difficult and hazardous even in summer time. All walkers are urged to take basic precautions for their own safety and welfare.

- Carry a map and compass and ensure you know how to use them.
- Be properly equipped. Take waterproofs and spare warm clothing.
- Wear robust walking boots. Take an emergency pack including whistle, first aid kit, survival bag and extra rations.

Howling at the Moon

- Avoid wearing denims – they shrink when wet and do not dry easily.
- Plan your route properly. Be aware of escape routes in the event of an accident. If walking alone leave a route card.
- Check the local weather forecast.
- Know your limitations. Do not tackle walks beyond your fitness, training or experience.

Be familiar with the Mountain Code.

The Mountain Code restates many of those points and adds a few new ones:

- Know how to use, and carry a map and compass.
- Know the weather signs and local forecast.
- Plan within your capabilities.
- Know simple first aid and the symptoms of exposure.
- Take waterproofs and a fleece.
- Ensure someone knows your planned route.
- Keep alert all day!

Chapter 10

Route Assessment

An accurate and detailed assessment of your proposed hike is important because, with the route data contained in the following chapter, it will inform your decisions on equipment, skills, clothing and food.

Weather details are given for each month of the year using measurements taken at the Settle weather station. The average figures for each month give a good idea of what can expected during that month, while the record highs and lows give an idea of what the weather is capable of in this part of the world. Temperature generally decreases 1C with every 100m in height gained (about 1°F for every 300ft).

The hours of daylight available, considered with the information on terrain and vegetation, should allow at least a rough calculation of probable daily mileage, and thus of food and accommodation requirements.

Route Assessment: The Pennine Way

Distance/Height
Distance: 423km
Ascent: 11,343m
Highest point: 893m (Cross Fell)
Lowest point: 120m (Hebden Bridge)

Climate (Settle – 130m ASL)

January

Temperature, average high:	4C / 38°F
Temperature, average low:	1C / 33°F
Temperature, record high:	12C / 54°F
Temperature, record low:	-8C / 19°F
Precipitation, total:	89mm / 3.5in
Precipitation type / frequency:	rain, snow / 12 days
Relative humidity:	87%
Wind, average:	20km/h / 12mph
Wind, record:	100km/h / 62mph
Sunshine:	3hrs/day
Sunrise / sunset:	0820 / 1617
Daylight:	7h 57m

February

Temperature, average high:	6C / 43°F
Temperature, average low:	0C / 32°F
Temperature, record high:	16C / 60°F
Temperature, record low:	-10C / 14°F
Precipitation, total:	78mm / 3in
Precipitation type / frequency:	rain, snow / 8 days
Relative humidity:	85%
Wind, average:	20km/h / 13mph
Wind, record:	83km/h / 52mph
Sunshine:	4hrs/day
Sunrise / sunset:	0729 / 1718
Daylight:	9h 49m

March

Temperature, average high:	8C / 47°F
Temperature, average low:	2C / 36°F
Temperature, record high:	18C / 65°F
Temperature, record low:	-10C / 14°F

Precipitation, total: 69mm / 2.7in
Precipitation type / frequency: rain, snow / 10 days
Relative humidity: 83%
Wind, average: 19km/h / 12mph
Wind, record: 83km/h / 52mph
Sunshine: 5hrs/day
Sunrise / sunset: 0621 / 1814
Daylight: 11h 53m

April
Temperature, average high: 10C / 51°F
Temperature, average low: 3C / 38°F
Temperature, record high: 24C / 75°F
Temperature, record low: -6C / 21°F
Precipitation, total: 62mm / 2.5in
Precipitation type / frequency: rain, snow / 8 days
Relative humidity: 81%
Wind, average: 16km/h / 10mph
Wind, record: 56km/h / 35mph
Sunshine: 8hrs/day
Sunrise / sunset: 0606 / 2012
Daylight: 14h 06m

May
Temperature, average high: 13C / 55°F
Temperature, average low: 6C / 42°F
Temperature, record high: 26C / 80°F
Temperature, record low: -5C / 22°F
Precipitation, total: 65mm / 2.6in
Precipitation type / frequency: rain / 6 days
Relative humidity: 78%
Wind, average: 14km/h / 9mph
Wind, record: 76km/h / 47mph
Sunshine: 8hrs/day
Sunrise / sunset: 0505 / 2106

Daylight: 16h 01m

June

Temperature, average high:	14C / 58°F
Temperature, average low:	9C / 47°F
Temperature, record high:	30C / 85°F
Temperature, record low:	1C / 34°F
Precipitation, total:	74mm / 3in
Precipitation type / frequency:	rain / 8 days
Relative humidity:	78%
Wind, average:	14km/h / 9mph
Wind, record:	74km/h / 46mph
Sunshine:	10hrs/day
Sunrise / sunset:	0437 / 2142
Daylight:	17h 05m

July

Temperature, average high:	19C / 66°F
Temperature, average low:	11C / 52°F
Temperature, record high:	30C / 86°F
Temperature, record low:	-5C / 23°F
Precipitation, total:	93mm / 3.5in
Precipitation type / frequency:	rain / 7 days
Humidity:	79%
Wind, average:	13km/h / 8mph
Wind, record:	48km/h / 30mph
Sunshine:	7hrs/day
Sunrise / sunset:	0459 / 2130
Daylight:	16h 31m

August

Temperature, average high:	19C / 66°F
Temperature, average low:	11C / 52°F
Temperature, record high:	32C / 89°F
Temperature, record low:	4C / 39°F

Route Assessment

Precipitation, total: 88mm / 3.5in
Precipitation type / frequency: rain / 8 days
Relative humidity: 80%
Wind, average: 13km/h / 8mph
Wind, record: 50km/h / 31mph
Sunshine: 7hrs/day
Sunrise / sunset: 0550 / 2034
Daylight: 14h 44m

September

Temperature, average high: 16C / 60°F
Temperature, average low: 9C / 48°F
Temperature, record high: 25C / 77°F
Temperature, record low: 1C / 34°F
Precipitation, total: 70mm / 2.8in
Precipitation type / frequency: rain / 7 days
Relative humidity: 82%
Wind, average: 13km/h / 8mph
Wind, record: 93km/h / 58mph
Sunshine: 6hrs/day
Sunrise / sunset: 0645 / 1920
Daylight: 12h 35m

October

Temperature, average high: 11C / 52°F
Temperature, average low: 7C / 44°F
Temperature, record high: 21C / 71°F
Temperature, record low: -4C / 25°F
Precipitation, total: 79mm / 3.1in
Precipitation type / frequency: rain / 9 days
Relative humidity: 86%
Wind, average: 15km/h / 9mph
Wind, record: 57km/h / 36mph
Sunshine: 5hrs/day
Sunrise / sunset: 0740 / 1807

Daylight: 10h 27m

November

Temperature, average high:	8C / 47°F
Temperature, average low:	4C / 38°F
Temperature, record high:	16C / 61°F
Temperature, record low:	-8C / 18°F
Precipitation, total:	82mm / 3.2in
Precipitation type / frequency:	rain, snow / 9 days
Relative humidity:	88%
Wind, average:	17km/h / 10mph
Wind, record:	69km/h / 43mph
Sunshine:	3hrs/day
Sunrise / sunset:	0740 / 1606
Daylight:	8h 26m

December

Temperature, average high:	5C / 41°F
Temperature, average low:	3C / 37°F
Temperature, record high:	14C / 56°F
Temperature, record low:	-8C / 18°F
Precipitation, total:	89mm / 3.5in
Precipitation type / frequency:	rain, snow / 11 days
Relative humidity:	89%
Wind, average:	17km/h / 11mph
Wind, record:	80km/h / 49mph
Sunshine:	4hrs/day
Sunrise / sunset:	0823 / 1545
Daylight:	7h 21m

The prevailing wind is from the west. The Pennines experience more than twice the usual UK average rainfall.

Footing

Muddy, uneven farm tracks and footpaths. Very boggy

on the moors. Mostly upland peat bogs with some farmland at lower levels.

Vegetation

The higher levels are mostly moorland comprising heather, bracken and grass.

The lower levels are farmland, mostly grass.

The path is a waymarked National Trail so vegetation density should not be an issue.

The main allergens are pollens. Their peak release periods are:

    Grass pollen: June and July.
    Tree pollen: mid-February to mid-July.
    Weed pollen: May to mid-August.

Maps needed

Harvey's 1:40,000: Pennine Way South, Pennine Way Central and Pennine Way North, or,

Ordnance Survey 1:50,000 Landranger: sheets 74, 80, 86, 87, 91, 92, 98, 103, 109 and 110, or,

Ordnance Survey 1:25,000 Explorer: sheets 1, 2, 16, 19, 21, 30, 31, 41, 42, 43 and 288.

Navigation aids

Visibility: the terrain is mostly open so visibility is good (weather permitting).

Topographical relief: for periods the route follows rivers and crosses identifiable hills.

The quality of trail tread is good where paths are paved, moderate on lower aspects and poor through higher moorland peat bogs where these are unpaved.

The trail is waymarked with the National Trail acorn symbol.

This is a well-used social trail particularly towards the southern end. The path is also well-used near villages in the

National Parks.

Sun exposure
There is little tree cover or other natural shade throughout the route.

Water availability
Water is readily available from campsites, pubs, public conveniences and streams/rivers. Consider treating water from streams/rivers.

Problematic wildlife
None.

Remoteness
This walk contains long, remote stretches away from busy roads or towns with services, particularly in Northumberland (a 43km stretch from Byrness to Kirk Yetholm).

Bogs, long distances and steep slopes all present natural barriers to self-rescue.

There is little or no mobile phone reception from:
> Horton-in-Ribblesdale to Hawes (and just beyond Hawes) (23km),
> Thwaite to Bowes Moor (20km),
> Langdon Beck to Garrigill (52km),
> Once Brewed to Bellingham (22km),
> Byrness to Kirk Yetholm (47km).

Coverage is poor in all low-lying areas.

Natural hazards
Bogs, bad weather, fog, heavy rain.

Chapter 11

Route Data

In this chapter, the route of the Pennine Way is described from south to north. When walking, find your location on the path and then refer to the data sheet. By that method you will be able to plan ahead in order to re-provision, visit interesting sites, camp, etc.

For each location, distances are shown in bold. Distance is shown from the last location and cumulatively from the start of the walk (in brackets), in both kilometres and miles. The location name is shown in italics, followed by its facilities, then places of interest, thus:

Km from last (cum km) / Miles from last (cum miles)
Place name
Facilities.
Places of interest.

> Indented entries are off the trail.

Shops, pubs, post offices, etc., sometimes change their opening hours and the services they offer, so if you intend to depend heavily upon one or more facilities, check before you leave!

The following abbreviations are used:
ATM: automatic teller machine (cash machine).

Howling at the Moon

       B&B: bed and breakfast establishment.
       PH: public house (pub).
       PO: Post Office.
       WC: public toilet (often with drinking water available).
       YHA: Youth Hostel Association (although no age limit).

An "off licence" is a shop licensed to sell intoxicating liquor for consumption off the premises only.

The opening hours of grocery shops are shown in the 24 hour format where known (Bank Holidays may vary).

A six figure Ordnance Survey grid reference is given to assist with the location of any facility where its location is not immediately obvious.

Route Data: The Pennine Way

0.0km (0.0km cumulative) / 0mi (0mi cumulative)
Edale
PHs x 2, campsites: 1) Fieldhead Camp Site (124,856); 2) Coopers Camp and Caravan Site, New Fold Farm (123,859) (N-most site at Edale), 3) Waterside Farm, Barber Booth Rd (114,848).

2.2km (2.2km) / 1.4mi (1.4mi)
Upper Booth
Campsite: Upper Booth Farm (102,852).

3.6km (5.8km) / 2.2mi (3.6mi)
Kinder Low

12.4km (18.2km) / 7.7mi (11.3mi)
Bleaklow Head

Route Data

7.2km (25.4km) / 4.5mi (15.8mi)
Crowden
Campsite: Crowden Camping and Caravanning Club Site, Woodhead Rd (072,993).

10.4km (35.8km) / 6.5mi (22.2mi)
A635 road.

7.6km (43.4km) / 4.7mi (27.0mi)
A62 road.
Campsite and PH: The Carriage House, Standedge Caravan and Campsite, Manchester Rd (027,102 - 700m north-east of route at 342m spot height just past reservoir). PH 400m north-east of route.

3.6km (47.0km) / 2.2mi (29.2mi)
A640 road.

3.6km (50.6km) / 2.2mi (31.4mi)
M62 motorway.

4.4km (55.0km) / 2.7mi (34.1mi)
A58 road, The White House.
PH.

> **6.8km (61.8km) / 4.2mi (38.4mi)**
> 1km north-west of route
> *Mankinholes*
> Campsite: Cross Farm (960, 239), YHA, PH.

> **5.6km (67.4km) / 3.5mi (41.9mi)**
> 1.5km east of route
> *Hebden Bridge*
> Shops: 1) Co-op, 41 Market St, Mon-Sat 0700-2200,

Sun 1100-1700, (990,272), 2) Spar, 12 Crown St, Mon-Sat 0700-2300, Sun 0700-2230, (992,273); PHs, cafés, PO, camping shop (Mountain Wild, Crown St), chemists, ATM, WC.

1.6km (69km) / 1.0mi (42.9mi)
Badgerfields
Campsite: Badger Fields Farm (968,276).

0.8km (69.8km) / 0.5mi (43.4mi)
600m west of route
Jack's Bridge
PH, (campsite closed).

0.8km (70.6km) / 0.5mi (43.9mi)
Colden
Campsite: High Gate Farm (963,288) and May's Aladdin's Cave shop, 0700-2100 every day.

1.2km (71.8km) / 0.7mi (44.6mi)
800m east of route
Coppy
Pennine Camp and Caravan Site, High Greenwood House (969,307).

3.6km (75.4km) / 2.2mi (46.9mi)
200m east of route
PH.

7.6km (83.0km) / 4.7mi (51.6mi)
The Height
Campsite closed.

Route Data

1.2km (84.2km) / 0.7mi (52.3mi)
600m east of route
PH.

0.6km (84.8km) / 0.4mi (52.7mi)
Ponden
Campsites: 1) The Mill, Scar Top Road - across dam, 200m north of route (995,373), 2) Ponden House (990,370).

9.2km (94.0km) / 5.7mi (58.4mi)
Cowling
"Village Local" shop, Colne Rd (974,432), campsite: Winterhouse Barn, Colne Rd (969,429), chemist, fish and chip shop (874,432), PH, WC.

4.0km (98.0km) / 2.5mi (60.9mi)
Lothersdale
PH, campsite: Lynmouth, Dale End (961,460).

10.4km (108.4km) / 6.5mi (67.4mi)
East Marton
PH, campsite: Sawley House (908,509).

4.4km (112.8km) / 2.7mi (70.1mi)
Gargrave
Shop: Co-op, High St, 0700-2200 every day (932,543), chemist; campsite: Eshton Road Caravan Site (935,546); PHs, PO, café, WC.

6.8km (119.6km) / 4.2mi (74.3mi)
Airton
Bunkhouse: Friends Meeting House and Barn, across bridge, first building on left (903,592), café.

3.0km (122.6km) / 1.9mi (76.2mi)
Skellands
Caravan site closed.

1.0km (123.6km) / 0.6mi (76.8mi)
600m west of route
Kirkby Malham
PH.

2.0km (125.6km) / 1.2mi (78.0mi)
Malham
Campsite: Townhead Farm - 200m north of Malham (899,633), PHs x 2, PO, café, WC, National Park Visitor Centre, tea van at Gordale bridge, YHA - next to Lister Arms PH (902,630), bunkhouse: Hill Top Farm, Back Lane (898,631).

1.4km (127.0km) / 0.9mi (78.9mi)
Malham Cove

11.2km (138.2km) / 7.0mi (85.9mi)
Fountains Fell
662m high.

11.4km (149.6km) / 7.1mi (93.0mi)
Horton-in-Ribblesdale
Campsite: Holme Farm (804,728); bunkhouses: 1) The Golden Lion PH, opposite the church (809,722), 2) 3 Peaks Bunkhouse, next to Golden Lion; PH, café, WC.

9.6km (159.2km) / 6.0mi (98.9mi)
Cam End
Path turns north-east.

Route Data

12.8km (172.0km) / 8.0mi (106.9mi)
Hawes
Shop: Spar, Market Place Main St, Mon-Fri 0800-1800, Sat 0800-1930, Sun 0900-1700 (872,898); campsites: 1) Blackburn Farm and Trout Fishery (875,894), 2) Bainbridge Ings (880,895); YHA (Lancaster Terrace - just off B6255 road), chemist, ATMs, PO, PHs, cafés, fish and chip shop, WC.

2.6km (174.6km) / 1.6mi (108.5mi)
Hardraw
PH x 2, café, campsites: 1) Old Hall Cottage, (866,913), 2) Public site behind The Green Dragon Inn, managed by the Heritage Centre (868,913); tearoom, Hardraw Force.

7.8km (182.4km) / 4.8mi (113.3mi)
Great Shunner Fell
716m high.

5.6km (188.0km) / 3.5mi (116.8mi)
Thwaite
PH, café.
1km east of route: campsite: Usha Gap (902,979).

5.2km (193.2km) / 3.2mi (120.0mi)
Keld
Campsites: 1) Park House (1km west of route, 887,015), 2) Rukins Park Lodge campsite (300m west of route, 893,012); café, WC.

2.0km (195.2km) / 1.3mi (121.3mi)
Haw Shaws Hill
200m east of route: café.

Howling at the Moon

4.4km (199.6km) / 2.7mi (124.0mi)
Tan Hill
PH - allows camping (897,067).

8.8km (208.4km) / 5.5mi (129.5mi)
Trough Heads
Path splits. Bowes Loop to Bowes, adds 6km: PH, PO, tiny shop, campsite closed.

2.0km (210.4km) / 1.2mi (130.7mi)
A66 road.
Pennine Way underpass.

6.0km (216.4km) / 3.7mi (134.4mi)
Baldersdale

1.2km (217.6km) / 0.8mi (135.2mi)
High Birk Hat
Visitor Centre.

> **8.8km (226.4km) / 5.5mi (140.7mi)**
> 800m east of route
> *Bowbank*
> Campsite: Highside Farm, Bowbank (947, 239).

0.4km (226.8km) / 0.2mi (140.9mi)
Step Ends
Campsite: Dale View Caravan Park (947,247).

> **0.4km (227.2km) / 0.2mi (141.1mi)**
> 500m east of route
> *Middleton-in-Teesdale*
> Shops: 1) Co-op, Chapel Row (948,254) 0700-22200 every day, 2) Armitage General Store, Horse Market

Route Data

(946,256); café, chemist, PH, ATM, fish and chip shop, PO.

6.0km (233.2km) / 3.8mi (144.9mi)
Low Force

2.8km (236.0km) / 1.7mi (146.6mi)
High Force

4.8km (240.8km) / 3.0mi (149.6mi)
800m east of route
Langdon Beck
YHA (Forest-in-Teesdale).

12.8km (253.6km) / 8.0mi (157.6mi)
High Cup

6.8km (260.4km) / 4.2mi (161.8mi)
Dufton
Campsite: Grandie Caravan Park (689,251), YHA, PH, café.

10.0km (270.4km) / 6.2mi (168.0mi)
Great Dun Fell
848m high.

1.0km (271.4km) / 0.6mi (168.6mi)
Little Dun Fell
842m high.

2.4km (273.8km) / 1.5mi (170.1mi)
Cross Fell
893m - highest point on the Pennine Way.

Howling at the Moon

1.8km (275.6km) / 1.1mi (171.2mi)
Greg's Hut
Bothy.

9.8km (285.4km) / 6.1mi (177.3mi)
Garrigill
Camping: Garrigill Village Hall (745,416) - Emily, 01434 647516, also bunkhouse; PH; PO/shop (745,415); WC, café.

7.6km (293.0km) / 4.7mi (182.0mi)
Alston
Shops: 1) Co-op, Market Place, 0700-2200 every day (718,466), 2) Spar, Townfoot, 0600-2200 every day (717,466); campsite: Tyne Willows Caravan Site, Station Road (716,467); Alston YHA, The Firs (717,462); PH, café, WC, PO, ATM, chemist, outdoor shop.

9.6km (302.6km) / 6.0mi (188.0mi)
Slaggyford

>**2.4km (305.0km) / 1.5mi (189.5mi)**
>400m east of route
>*Knarsdale*
>PH.
>
>**4.8km (309.8km) / 3.0mi (192.5mi)**
>1km east of route
>*Halton Lea Gate*
>PO.
>
>**9.2km (319.0km) / 5.7mi (198.2mi)**
>1km east of route
>*Bankfoot*
>Campsite, PH.

Route Data

0.8km (319.8km) / 0.5mi (198.7mi)
1km east of route
Greenhead
Campsite, PH, café.

1.4km (321.2km) / 0.9mi (199.6mi)
Hadrian's Wall
Camping barn: Holmhead (659,660), café.

0.0km (321.2km) / 0.0mi (199.6mi)
2km west of route
Gilsland
Shop: Gilsland Village Store, B6318 (635,664), café, PH, WC.

1.0km (322.2km) / 0.6mi (200.2mi)
Thirwall Castle
Café, WC.

5.4km (327.6km) / 3.4mi (203.6mi)
Cawfields
Water point, WC. PH 700m south of route, campsite 1.3km south of route (Herdin Hill Farm (714,654)).

1.6km (329.2km) / 1.0mi (204.6mi)
1km south of route
Caw Gap
Hadrian's Wall Camping and Caravan Site (728,659).

2.0km (331.2km) / 1.2mi (205.8mi)
1km south of route
Green Slack
Campsite: Winshields Farm, Military Rd (744,668).

1.0km (332.2km) / 0.6mi (206.4mi)
Once Brewed
PH, water point, WC.

3.2km (335.4km) / 2.0mi (208.4mi)
1.2 km east of route
Housesteads Fort
WC, water point, café.

8.2km (343.6km) / 5.1mi (213.5mi)
2km north-west of route
Stonehaugh
Campsite: Stonehaugh Campsite, The Old Farmhouse, Stonehaugh (794,764).

8.4km (352.0km) / 5.2mi (218.7mi)
200m west of route
Shitlington Crags
Shitlington Crag Bunk House (828,808).

3.2km (355.2km) / 2.0mi (220.7mi)
Eals Burn, B6320 road.
Campsite: Bellingham Camping and Caravanning Club Site (835,825).

1.6km (356.8km) / 1.0mi (221.7mi)
Bellingham
Shop: Co-op, 2-3 Parkside Place, 0700-2200 every day (839,833); campsite: Desmesne Farm (841,831) = campsite and YHA bunkhouse; PO, ATM, café, PH, WC.

21.2km (378.0km) / 13.2mi (234.9mi)
Blakehopeburnhaugh
WC.

Route Data

1.4km (379.4km) / 0.9mi (235.8mi)
Cottonshopeburnfoot
Border Forest Caravan Park (779,014) – no tents accepted.

2.0 (381.4km) / 1.2mi (237.0mi)
Byrness
Forest View Inn, 6-8 Otterburn Green, Byrness.

26.4km (407.8km) / 16.4mi (253.4mi)
1.8km north-east of route
The Cheviot
815m, highest peak in the Cheviot Hills.

14.8km (422.6km) / 9.2mi (262.6mi)
Kirk Yetholm
Hostel: Friends of Nature House (826,282); PH.

0.0km / 0.0mi
800m west of finish point
Town Yetholm
Shop: Yetholm Village Shop, High St (819,281); campsite: Kirkfield Caravan Site, Grafton Road (822,283); PH.

Index

A

A Pennine Journey, book by Alfred Wainwright, 79
Aire, River, 75, 76
Alston, 112, 113, 116, 119, 160

B

Backpacking, lightweight, 2, 3, 6
Bellingham, 125-127, 150, 162
Blakehopeburnhaugh, 129, 162
Bleaklow Head, 58, 152
Bowes Moor, 150
Brontës, The, 69, 70
Byrness, 113, 129-130, 131, 150, 163

C

Cam End, 85, 156
Carriage House, The, 60, 63, 133, 153
Cauldron Snout, 107, 108
Cawfields, 161
Chapel Jane, 37
Cheviot Hills, 113, 129, 130, 132, 134-135
Colden, 66, 154

Cornish Coast Path, 30-51
Cornwall, 30-51
Cow Green, 107-109, 112
Cowling, 70-71, 155
Cross Fell, 111-113, 143, 159
Crowden, 153

D

Dufton, 107, 110-111, 159

E

East Marton, 73, 155
Edale, 54, 139, 152

F

Fitzroy Barometer, 50
Food for backpacking, 3, 16-22, 25, 124, 143
Fountains Fell, 77, 156

G

Gargrave, 73, 155
Garrigill, 112, 113-116, 150, 160
God's Bridge, 103
Great Dun Fell, 112, 159
Great Shunner Fell, 88-89, 157
Greg's Hut, 111, 112, 160
Gwennap Head (day marks for shipping), 45

H

Hadrian's Wall, 121-123, 130, 141, 161
Hannah's Meadow, 105-106
Hauxwell, Hannah, 105-106
Hawes, 85, 86, 87, 88, 150, 157
Hayle, 30-31, 38
Hebden Bridge, 66-67, 143, 153
High Cup, 107, 110, 159
High Force, 107-108, 159
High Gate Farm, 67-68, 154
Hillaby, John, 22-23, 67, 75, 76, 103, 108-109, 116, 123, 125
Horneystead Farm, 124-125
Horton-in-Ribblesdale, 78-79, 83, 150, 154
Housesteads Fort, 122-123, 162
Huddersfield Canal Company, 60, 61

I

Imperial Chemical Industries Ltd, 108

J

Journey Through Britain, book by John Hillaby, 22

K

Kielder Forest, 128-129
Keld, 90, 157
Kinder Low, 152
Kinder Trespass, 56-57
Kirk Yetholm, 61, 132, 134, 135, 139, 150, 163

L

Lamorna Cove, 49
Land's End, 22, 30, 44
Langdon Beck, 150
Lawrence, D.H., 35-36
Lelant, 31
Little Dun Fell, 159
Long Pack, The Story of the, 126-127
Lothersdale, 71, 155
Low Force, 107, 159
"Lynmouth", 71-73, 155

M

Malham, 75-77, 156
Malham Cove, 76, 77, 156
Man-cave, 80
Mankinholes, 153
May's Aladdin's Cave, 67-68, 154
Merry Maidens Stone Circle, 47-48
Middleton-in-Teesdale, 106-107, 158
Mithraism, 122
Mobile phone reception, 150
Mousehole, 50

N

Newcastle and Carlisle Railway, 117
North Pennines, The, 93-120
Northumberland, 121-135

O

Once Brewed, 150

P

Peak District, The, 54-62
Pen-y-ghent, 78-79
Pennine Way, History of, 61
Penzance, 30, 38, 50
Phone reception, 150
Ponden, 70, 155
Ponden Hall, 70
Ponden House, 70, 155
Porthcurno, 46-47

R

Runnel Stone, The, 45

S

Shipwrecks, 36, 45
Shitlington Crags, 125, 162
Slack Bottom, 67, 68
Slaggyford, 119, 160
South Pennines, The, 63-74
South Tynedale Railway, 117-118
South-west Coast Path, 30
St Ives, 31-32
St Levan, 46
St Levan's Well, 46
Stephenson, Tom, 61
Stoodley Pike, 65, 66

Swaledale, 90

T

Tan Hill, 91-94, 157
Tan Hill Inn, 91-94, 157
Teesdale, 106, 107-108, 159
Telegraph, 46-47
Thwaite, 89, 90, 150, 157
Town Yetholm, 163
Trail Magic, 124
Treveal Stone Circle, 34

W

Wainwright, Alfred, 79, 91, 94, 102, 107, 114, 119, 120 123, 135
Warcop military training area, 109
Wensleydale, 88
White House, The, 64, 153

Y

Yorkshire Dales, The, 75-92

Z

Zennor, 34-36

About the Author

John Davison started hiking and camping on school trips and in the Scouts, during the early 1970s. Exploring new places, meeting new people and discovering how the two interrelate is an interest which has never left him.

John is a Fellow of the Royal Geographical Society and he lives in Essex, UK.

Other books by John Davison

Every Day Above a New Horizon

In 1878 Robert Louis Stevenson, the author of Treasure Island and Kidnapped, walked across the south of France with a donkey. His plan was to write an account of his journey and to use the proceeds to fund a trip across the Atlantic to re-join the love of his life in the USA.

Inspired by Stevenson's account, John Davison finds himself constrained by his job in London and by his family commitments. Far from making things better, a series of short hiking trips in the UK only serve to fan the flame until, finally, the opportunity presents itself.

John sets off in Stevenson's footsteps, sensibly without the donkey, through blazing sun and driving rain, across one of the least populated parts of Europe; encountering kind, generous people, leavened with the occasional idiot, meeting them all with an keen eye and a dry sense of humour as he heads towards journey's end: the golden city down on the plain.

This is the art of the possible: John tells the story of one man's journey with just enough "how-to" to inspire you to start your own...

If you are old enough, you'll remember the Apollo space missions taking off from Cape Kennedy. And you might remember the countdown, 10, 9, 8 and so on, right down to zero! At that point, right when you might have expected the rocket to soar up into the sky, nothing happened. Well, nothing obvious happened. In reality, of course, there was lots going on. All systems were go, the engines had fired and were now building up power to thrust the huge rocket into space. At zero! there wasn't much to see, but we all knew that something momentous was about to happen.

So it was in the back bar of the Ardlui Hotel. There wasn't anything obvious to see, but everyone knew that something was going to happen...

Reviewers say:

"A truly inspiring read, written from the heart of a man with enthusiasm and passion for walking."

"A great story teller."

"Highly recommended not only as a traveller's tale but also a guide to wild camping."

"A great book to have in your bag."

A Spring Ramble

Walking the Offa's Dyke Path

Offa's Dyke.

The border between England and Wales.

1,200 years old and 177 miles long.

More ascent than Everest.

The most impressive monument of its kind in Europe, now a national walking trail.

The present-day peace and tranquillity of this beautiful, remote area belie its turbulent past. Follow the walk from sea to sea, past castles, battlegrounds and ancient churches, over mountains and alongside rivers. Discover the history of this fascinating, enchanting region and some of the personalities who ruled, fought, built, farmed, robbed, wrote, painted and campaigned here.

The English Coast to Coast Walk

What it's really like and how to do it

Alfred Wainwright's genius was in constructing a walk which is demanding but which constantly stimulates. He knew the north of England well and he loved it.

AW applied that knowledge and that love to devise a route which covers the most beautiful parts of England, but which does so in a way which surprises and delights throughout its length. I was to discover that it's difficult to be bored on this walk. Just as you begin to get tired of the ups and downs of the Lake District, you find yourself crossing flat grassland and heading into the Pennines. If the moors start to pall, don't worry: in a few hours you'll find yourself dropping down through farms and villages. I was to pass sites of human activity dating from the prehistoric to the present day and ranging from the pastoral to the industrial.

Not for nothing is this one of the most famous walks in the world.

Connect with Me

For help planning your own trip, check my website at

www.johndavison.strikingly.com

If you have any questions, email me via the "Contact" button and I'll do my best to answer them.

Keep up-to-date with my latest adventure by following me on Twitter: @bootsonthehill.

Happy trekking!

Printed in Great Britain
by Amazon